COURAGE HAS NO COLOR

THE TRUE STORY OF THE TRIPLE NICKLES

COURAGE HAS NO COLOR

THE TRUE STORY OF THE TRIPLE NICKLES

America's First Black Paratroopers

TANYA LEE STONE

CANDLEWICK PRESS

First paperback edition 2013

Library of Congress Catalog Card Number 2012942315
ISBN 978-0-7636-5117-6 (hardcover)
ISBN 978-0-7636-6548-7 (paperback)

22 23 24 CCP 14 13 12

Printed in Shenzhen, Guangdong, China

This book was typeset in Baskerville.

Candlewick Press
99 Dover Street
Somerville, Massachusetts 02144

visit us at www.candlewick.com

To all the brave, patriotic people
who put their lives on the line for
their nation, no matter the personal
cost. And for Walter Morris,
without whom the Triple Nickles
might never have been.

T. L. S.

"Soldiers were fighting the world's worst racist, Adolph Hitler, in the world's most segregated army."

—Stephen Ambrose, historian

"Racial intolerance is undemocratic and un-American and can be defended on no intelligent grounds. Its existence in any degree in this country at a time when we are sacrificing our blood and our treasure for the destruction of fascism is an embarrassing contradiction; for racial intolerance is an element of fascism."

—Evans Fordyce Carlson, colonel,
United States Marine Corps, 1945

CONTENTS

Ashley Bryan, now an award-winning children's book author and illustrator, found a way to paint and draw during his time as a stevedore in the Army's 502nd Port Battalion in World War II. This painting, done in France, shows a signalman in Ashley's company.

FOREWORD

Perhaps you may have read a book, a true account of an event that parallels your own experience. Tanya Lee Stone's story of the Triple Nickles, a story I did not know, does this for me. This story evokes so deeply what I have lived that the emotional passage for me was at times overwhelming. You see, I am a black veteran of World War II. I was drafted at the age of nineteen, out of art college in New York City, into a port battalion. I found my way of insisting on my desire to grow as an artist despite the exhausting work of a stevedore in the Army. From basic training to work on the docks of Boston and then Glasgow, Scotland, and into the surprise invasion of Normandy at Omaha Beach, I survived—with a sketch pad in my gas mask and helped by the warm support of the men in my company. Reading this story moved me to take out some of the artwork I had done during the war and share it with Tanya.

As I read the story of First Sergeant Walter Morris and these black paratroopers, my steps and my mood kept me as one of them. All that you will read in this account is what we experienced. How does one survive and outlast the racism that was our daily fare at that time? You will read of how Morris led the men in his company to tap the essential humanity within, transcend discrimination, and overcome the odds. It is an inspiring story of how one fights to assure that decency and pride survive.

Through her telling of the Triple Nickles' story, Tanya Lee Stone presents an all-inclusive picture of our struggle to realize the democracy we as Americans are still working toward. You will be caught up in the rhythmic pacing of events that underscore how the Triple Nickles served as a beautiful symbol of what we are as humans, not just as Americans. Despite the indecencies directed toward them *because* of color, the black paratroopers held rather to the decencies of people who honored their gifts of service to the nation *despite* color.

This is a moving story, touching, extraordinary. It is an important book.

—Ashley Bryan

A student from The Parachute School jumps near the Drop Zone that was later used by the Triple Nickles test platoon. July 24, 1943.

CHAPTER ONE

COURAGE HAS NO COLOR

What is it like to jump out of an airplane?

Imagine.

You are a paratrooper suiting up for a jump. Guys on either side of you are doing the same. One jokes about having a dream that the chutes didn't open. Another one says he's glad everyone paid their insurance.

You stand strong, even though you are loaded down with a hundred pounds of equipment strapped to your body — main chute, reserve chute, and combat gear.

The jumpmaster walks down the line, inspecting each of you, making sure you are properly fitted. Your life depends on it.

The joking stops.

The jumpmaster commands, "Load."

In jump order, your line of troopers — your stick — climbs into the plane. You follow the trooper in front of you to your spot and sit.

Now you are in the air, on the way to the Drop Zone. You're chatting with your buddies above the noise of the plane. "Puke buckets" are always on board, but you don't need one today.

Twenty minutes from the Drop Zone, it's time to get serious.

The red warning light near the door turns on.

The jumpmaster stands and shouts, "Get ready!"

He walks down the line, alerting each jumper with a word in the ear and a touch on the shoulder, making sure each and every man hears him.

You shuffle forward, sticking close to the man in front of you. The man in back of you does the same.

You watch as the troopers in front of you follow each command, quickly disappearing one by one out the open door of the plane.

And now it's your turn.

"Stand in the door!"

Nothing separates you from the sky but one last sliver of floor. The tip of your left boot hangs slightly over the edge.

The wind whips. The white is blinding, bright.

Adrenaline pulses through you.

You look down at a brown and green patchwork quilt of open fields and thickets of trees.

Nothing separates you from the sky but one last sliver of floor.

The roar of the engine pulses with the pounding of your heart.

You are over the Drop Zone. It's time.

The jumpmaster bellows, "GO!"

You jump.

You force yourself to focus. Count.

"One thousand, two thousand, three thousand . . ."

Your hand is on the reserve chute, ready if you need it.

Thwap! Your main chute opens, and the line snaps tight. You are floating
     down . . .

          down . . .

               down . . .

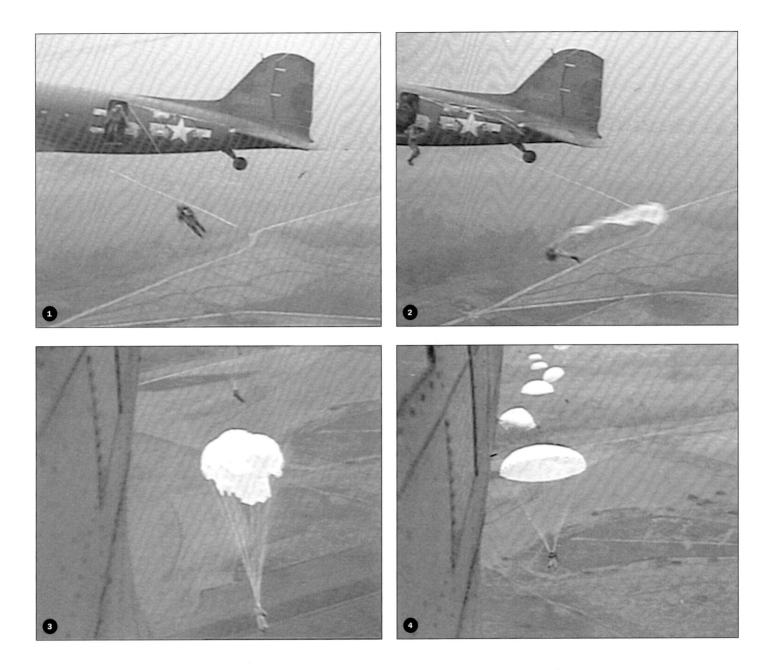

The rumble of the plane and the jumpmaster's shouts are gone.

Your ears fill with a hush unlike any other.

Extreme quiet.

Looking down, feet together, you see the ground through the tiny ∨ space where the toes of your boots almost touch.

Looking up, you see the reassuring inside of your open chute.

Stills from a video of the 555th on a training jump in 1944.

1) Jumper exits and next jumper prepares to follow

2) Static line pulls the parachute from the pack tray on jumper's back

3) Parachute begins to take shape

4) Parachutes are fully deployed

Looking out, you see the other jumpers' chutes falling with yours like jellyfish swimming through a sea of sky.

The ground gets closer, rushing toward you as if wanting to swallow you whole.

For an instant, your billowy chute seems like it might cradle you on impact.

Then you hit the ground. Hard. *Thud!*

Even a perfect landing sends shock waves rolling up through the soles of your feet all the way to your jaw, clapping it shut.

> **The ground gets closer, rushing toward you as if wanting to swallow you whole.**

What did it take to be a paratrooper in World War II? Specialized training, extreme physical fitness, courage, and—until the 555th Parachute Infantry Battalion (the Triple Nickles) was formed—white skin.

It is 1943. Americans are overseas fighting World War II to help keep the world safe from Adolf Hitler's tyranny, safe from injustice, safe from discrimination. Yet right here at home, people with white skin have rights that people with black skin do not.

What is courage? What is strength? Perhaps it is being ready to fight for your nation even when your nation isn't ready to fight for you.

Left: A jumper tugs the front side of his chute to move forward as the wind pushes him back. This is called pulling a front slip. Soon, he will put his feet together for a safe landing.

At the start of World War II, only one out of every 120 soldiers was black, and most were relegated to service duties. Here, Arnold R. Fesser, an oiler, maintains the moving parts of his ship's engine in October 1944.

CHAPTER TWO

SOLDIERS, NOT SERVANTS

Walter Morris stood tall and lean. He was born in Waynesboro, Georgia, in 1921. His family moved north to Newark, New Jersey, when he was just four years old. But Walter's mother sent him back to Georgia to live with his uncle during high school to get him away from the gangs and other bad influences in Newark. Soon after graduation, he joined the Army.

By the fall of 1943, Morris was a first sergeant, in charge of the Service Company of The Parachute School (TPS) at Fort Benning, Georgia. He took his responsibilities seriously but was quick with a smile. The warm look in his eyes put people at ease. He was well liked by his men.

The Army had begun training parachutists only three years earlier. The job of the men in the Service Company was simple: to guard the facility. Every day, guard duty began at four o'clock p.m., when the white paratrooper students finished their training and left the fields.

Through the night, until eight the next morning, these black servicemen made their rounds. They patrolled past the supply shed, past the jump towers, past the empty airfield, past the vacated exercise area.

Walter Morris poses with his wife, Ruby, and baby daughter, Patricia, at Fort Benning.

Morris's job as first sergeant was to make sure that the company commander's orders were being carried out so his 150 servicemen had what they needed—adequate food, clothing, and supplies—and did what they were supposed to. The men handled their job just fine. But they lacked the most important thing they needed: purpose.

The dull, repetitive, daily task of guarding The Parachute School was taking its toll on them. Their spirits were down. During their off time, they had little interest in doing much other than sleeping.

"As first sergeant, I had to do something about it," Morris said. He understood how his men felt.

These men were not alone. Most black soldiers in World War II were kept out of combat. Instead, the military often assigned them to service duties such as building roads, driving trucks, sweeping up, unloading cargo, cooking, doing laundry, serving meals, or guarding facilities. Of course, there is honor in any of these jobs. But less so if the job is forced upon a person, if one is not offered other options. As one soldier put it, "It is hard to identify one's self with fighting a war, when all one does is dig ditches."

Morris knew his men didn't feel much like soldiers. They weren't being given an opportunity to contribute to the war in a way that meant something to them. He wanted them "to act like soldiers, not servants."

Clarence Beavers served with Morris. Born and raised in New York City, Beavers was in the National Guard before the draft. Then, in 1941, he was drafted and went to Fort Benning in April 1943, serving as a company clerk. Beavers is a thoughtful man with a great grin. But his smile fades when he talks about wanting more: "We wanted to be a full partner within the war. We did not want to go through this war saying, 'I washed the dishes.' . . . I had a grandfather who ran away from his master as a slave and joined the Union Army and fought as a soldier in the Union Army. And here I am coming down almost a hundred years later and I cannot even fight in a war that's about to eat up the whole world."

The Right to Fight

The U.S. military has a long history of racial prejudice, from the Revolutionary War, the Civil War, and right up through World War II. Despite the fact that African-American soldiers had served the Army with distinction in World War I, there were outspoken and unfair criticisms about their abilities. In a book called *The Employment of Negro Troops*, considered an official part of U.S. Army history, author Ulysses Lee quotes white officers of all-black units from World War I saying, "The Negro should not be used as a combat soldier" and "The Negro must be rated as second class material, this due primarily to his inferior intelligence and lack of mental and moral qualifications." No matter how false, these were difficult statements to overcome.

By 1940, neither the Navy nor the Marines had room for blacks outside of service roles. And of the approximately 500,000 soldiers in the Army by the end of 1940, only a little more than 4,000 were black. These men were mostly in the 2nd Cavalry Division and the 92nd and 93rd Infantry Divisions, reactivated all-black divisions from World War I. (The 24th and 25th Infantry Regiments, which had remained active, were also folded into these divisions.)

Colonel Howard Donovan Queen, an African-American soldier who served in World War I and was later a commanding

Clarence Beavers was about to go overseas with a service unit when he got wind of a possible paratrooper opportunity at Fort Benning. He volunteered to go, but there were no training plans in place when he arrived. He was assigned to The Parachute School as a cadet, attached to the service company until training began.

"NATIONAL WAR AGENCIES, ARMY AND NAVY DEPARTMENTS URGE MORE EXTENSIVE USE OF NEGRO WORKERS IN WAR INDUSTRIES"..... NEWS ITEM

HE'S WILLING, HE'S CAPABLE, AND WE NEED HIM — USE HIM!!

During World War II, African-American artist Charles Alston was hired by the Office of War Information to create cartoons that would gain black support for the war effort. This 1943 cartoon depicts war agencies urging the use of black workers.

officer of the all-black 366th Regiment of the 92nd Infantry Division in World War II, said, "World War I [had been] one big racial problem for the Negro soldier. World War II was a racial nightmare. . . . The Negro soldier's first taste of warfare in World War II was on Army posts right here in his own country. This in its turn caused considerable confusion in the minds of the draftees as to who the enemy really was."

Black leaders had been fighting for the military to end segregation and increase opportunities for black soldiers. They wanted not only "the right to fight"; they also wanted to be treated as equals alongside white soldiers. In 1939, the Committee for the Participation of Negroes in National Defense was created, led by African-American scholar and historian Rayford W. Logan, who had left the Army during World War I because he was so disturbed by the discrimination he suffered as a soldier. Logan, accompanied by members of the National Association for the Advancement of Colored People (NAACP) and the black newspaper the *Pittsburgh Courier*, spoke to the House of Representatives Committee on Military Affairs to ask for the number of black military personnel to be increased.

Logan and his fellow advocates also wanted African-American soldiers to be used to their fullest instead of being limited to labor duties. They knew that, in order for this idea to work in practice, antisegregation and other nondiscrimination rules would need to be put into effect. White senators Sherman Minton (who became a Supreme Court justice), Robert Wagner (who ran for president in 1944), and Harry H. Schwartz (who also argued in favor of training black pilots) agreed and proposed amendments to the Selective Training and Service Bill. These amendments were rejected.

New York representative Hamilton Fish (whose grandfather had served as U.S. secretary of state after the Civil War) went back to the table and asked for an amendment stating that "draftees be selected in an impartial manner" and that "there should be no discrimination in either the selection or training of men." Although this amendment was approved, some Congress members did not believe it would be enough to end segregation in the military. President Roosevelt agreed and issued a press release on October 9, 1940, that supported some of what the black leaders wanted but also included many frustrating conditions.

For example, blacks were given more chances to be officers, but only of all-black units. The press release implied that segregation would continue because it had "been proved satisfactory over a long period of years." It also said that desegregation "would produce situations destructive to morale and detrimental to the preparation for national defense." In other words, putting black and white soldiers together would cause more trouble than it was worth and could be downright dangerous.

Humble and Sweet . . . or Angry Rebels

What explains this frame of mind? America was in the throes of change. Some regions still enforced racial separation, while in other areas, mainly large cities, pockets of people of different races coexisted peacefully. And although there had been migrations of blacks from the South to the North in the past—especially after the Civil War and World War I—at the onset of World War II, southern blacks and whites flocked to cities in the West, Midwest, and North, where the war industry was offering employment. While people in these areas tended to be more accepting of blacks than those in the South, these regions were not without problems. Some tensions arose because whites suddenly had to share resources such as jobs and housing with large numbers of new black residents. Where resources were limited, and ideas of white superiority lingered, clashes broke out.

July 1939. An African-American man drinks from a water cooler marked COLORED in Oklahoma City.

Segregation was still common practice in the South—in jobs, schools, housing, transportation, and public areas such as swimming pools, movie theaters, restaurants, and hotels. Blacks who didn't follow the rules were in danger. In Eustis, Florida, a little boy named George Starling grew up hearing horror stories of lynching and other violent acts inflicted upon blacks for something as small as drinking from the wrong water fountain—or for no reason at all. He told Isabel Wilkerson, who wrote about Starling's experiences in her book *The Warmth of Other Suns,* how he felt: "It seemed as if the whole world was crazy. . . . All this stepping off the sidewalk, not looking even in the direction of a white woman, the sirring and ma'aming and waiting until all the white people had been served before buying your ice cream cone, with violence and even death awaiting any misstep."

Stereotypical ideas about blacks came through loud and clear in the media, too. Movies and radio programs categorized African Americans as humble and sweet servants to white bosses, as clowns and jesters happy to entertain, or as angry rebels who needed to be put in their place. In 1915, D. W. Griffith's film *The Birth of a Nation* portrayed a southern pre–Civil War family getting along well with their slaves who "contentedly pick cotton" and "dance and perform for their master." Later in the film, though, the Civil War disrupts this happy scene and the blacks rebel and break free from these roles, but often violently or crudely and never with dignity. Griffith's movie was popular with white audiences, but the NAACP protested it, saying that it harmed society's view of blacks.

Gone with the Wind, the next big movie about the Civil War, came out in 1939. It reinforced more black stereotypes, especially through the character of Mammy, the strong but loving servant who is so loyal to her mistress that she fights off black soldiers to protect the southern plantation she calls home. She even chooses to stay with Miss Scarlett after being set free when slavery is abolished. This "mammy" figure, often a heavyset black woman wearing a maid's uniform or a kerchief on her head, showed up repeatedly across media forms—in cartoons, songs, television shows, movies, and advertisements. All of these portrayals reflected the idea that black Americans were childish, backward, or dangerous—and certainly not equal to their white counterparts.

During segregation, movie houses like this one in Mississippi had a separate entrance that black patrons had to use.

Stereotypes in Early Movies and Advertising

Lena Horne was the first African American to sign a movie contract that promised not to cast her in negative roles. But then she guest-starred as herself and said, "They didn't make me into a maid, but they didn't make me into anything else either." Directors placed her in scenes that could be cut when shown in the South so Southerners wouldn't protest her non-subservient roles.

Stereotypes abound in *Gone with the Wind*. Offscreen, the black actors were banned from the premiere. Leading man Clark Gable threatened to boycott if Hattie McDaniel—who played Mammy—couldn't go. For her role, McDaniel became the first African American to win an Academy Award.

The Birth of a Nation depicts happy pre–Civil War slaves, while post-war scenes turn them into vicious rebels. The Ku Klux Klan (which advocates white supremacy through violence) is glorified as a heroic group that stifles the rebels. The film sparked a resurgence of the KKK.

Aunt Jemima was named after a song about a mammy, and the character became a trademark. She wore a head wrap associated with black female slaves, and the advertising campaign featured a former slave named Nancy Green, who made public appearances as Aunt Jemima. A fictional life for Aunt Jemima was created, which included her working on Colonel Higbee's Louisiana plantation, shown in this 1940s ad.

Coax as long as they might, guests at Colonel Higbee's plantation never could get from Aunt Jemima the flavor secret of those wonderful pancakes.

What Aunt Jemima would never tell them...she got her matchless flavor with a blend of four flours

Wheat, corn, rye and rice flours were blended in the treasured Aunt Jemima recipe to give the tenderest, best-tasting pancakes anyone ever had.

Today, Aunt Jemima Pancake Mix is faithful to that recipe. It's produced now, of course, with all the advantages of modern milling methods.

Over the years as other pancake mixes have come and gone, none ever made pancakes with such *flavor* as the Aunt Jemima brand. Really, it's true: You can't duplicate in a homemade batter or get with any other mix the matchless flavor of Aunt Jemima pancakes. For a special treat team up that flavor with fresh asparagus in the delightful springtime way shown here.

ASPARAGUS ROLL-UPS. Prepare pancakes according to Deluxe recipe on the Aunt Jemima package. Roll each hot pancake around several spears of cooked asparagus. Serve with cheese sauce. Garnish each roll-up with a strip of pimiento or sprinkle with paprika.

Who does this ad target — the black woman in the uniform being shown using bad grammar, or the person hiring her to wash the dishes? Hint: the consumer is not getting her hands wet. This 1930s GE ad assumes racial stereotypes that would not be tolerated today.

This 1930s Monel ad is a typical example of negative stereotyping. It uses an illustration, a form that allows the artist to further exaggerate the cliché of the black mammy character happy to serve the likely white owner of that brand-new water heater.

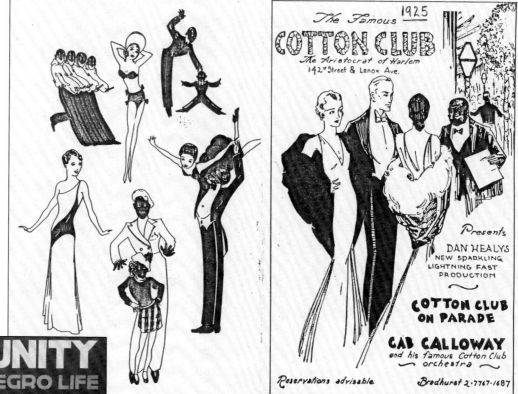

The Cotton Club (top) was open only to whites but offered a venue for some of the greatest black entertainers of the time, such as Duke Ellington, Ella Fitzgerald, and Nat King Cole. The magazine *Opportunity* (bottom) represented a new avenue for talented black writers and artists to be published.

No Discrimination . . . Because of Race, Creed, Color, or National Origin

Important positive changes were taking place. The NAACP, which worked with Rayford Logan on the Selective Training and Service Bill amendment, had grown from 9,000 to 90,000 members during World War I. By 1946, it would hit 500,000 members. Its publication, *The Crisis*, had an enormous readership, and the number of African-American newspapers, such as the *Chicago Defender,* New York's *Amsterdam News,* and the *Pittsburgh Courier,* was rapidly increasing.

These northern newspapers reached far and wide and were a powerful means of uniting people and alerting them to how life for African Americans was beginning to change in parts of the country. Readers learned, for example, that more jobs were

FDR's Black Cabinet, March 1938. Most were community leaders, not politicians. Front row, left to right: Dr. Ambrose Caliver, Dr. Roscoe C. Brown, Dr. Robert C. Weaver, Joseph H. Evans, Dr. Frank Horne, Mary McLeod Bethune, Lieutenant Lawrence A. Oxley, Dr. William J. Thompkins, Charles E. Hall, William I. Houston, Ralph E. Mizelle. Back row, left to right: Dewey R. Jones, Edgar Brown, J. Parker Prescott, Edward H. Lawson Jr., Arthur Weiseger, Alfred Edgar Smith, Henry A. Hunt, John W. Whitten, Joseph R. Houchins.

open to them in the North, even if blacks would not earn the same pay as whites. Southern blacks were encouraged to migrate north, where racism was certainly not gone but was a bit easier to stomach in light of more tolerable living conditions. When George Starling moved from Florida to New York during World War II, he got a job working as a coach attendant on a train. The white passengers still called him "boy," even though he was twenty-seven years old by then, and a tall, outspoken man. As Isabel Wilkerson describes it in *The Warmth of Other Suns*, "They could call him what they wanted on the train. He didn't like it, but it didn't define him. He lived in Harlem now and was free."

And then there was Franklin Delano Roosevelt (FDR), who was president from 1932 to 1945. At the suggestion of his wife, First Lady Eleanor Roosevelt, FDR put together a group, informally called the Black Cabinet, to help him understand what black Americans needed from their government. Some of his New Deal programs also helped create job opportunities for blacks. In 1941, civil rights leader A. Philip Randolph threatened a massive march on Washington unless Roosevelt agreed to integrate the Army and end racial discrimination in the defense industry. This industry was experiencing a huge rise in jobs because the military needed ships, aircraft, weapons, and other war-related supplies and services, but was giving most of these jobs to whites. FDR met with Randolph

"A STEP IN THE RIGHT DIRECTION!!"

In this 1943 cartoon, Alston highlights the supposed change in attitude toward black workers. Although his cartoons were intended to run in black newspapers, some editors refused because they felt the images did not reflect what was going on in reality.

and Walter White, head of the NAACP. He did not agree to integration, but he did issue Executive Order 8802, commonly called the Fair Employment Act, which prohibited discrimination in the defense industry. The Order said: "I do hereby reaffirm the policy of the United States that there shall be no discrimination in the employment of workers in defense industries or government because of race, creed, color, or national origin."

Of course, these few changes did not make racism and prejudice disappear. Some soldiers sent letters to the African-American newspapers in search of help, such as one addressed to the *Pittsburgh Courier:* "We have a lot of skilled workers here. . . . But, we are not classified by our skill. We're classified by color. If you're white you get the good jobs. And if you're colored you get a pick and shovel." The men who wrote the letter were afraid to sign their names for fear of worse treatment.

In another letter, sent to the secretary of war's office, a group of soldiers stationed at Camp McCoy, in Wisconsin, wrote: "On the post and off we are subjected to being called names. . . . When we report these things, they are overlooked. There is an inner tension growing among the men, they fell [*sic*] they would just as soon be in the guard house as in this slave camp."

The treatment of black soldiers stationed in the South was far worse than that in the North. Some black soldiers actually feared for their lives. From Jackson, Mississippi, a group of soldiers wrote to William H. Hastie. He was an African-American judge and scholar who had graduated first in his class from both high school and Amherst College and was dean of the Howard University Law School. Hastie had been asked to serve as the civilian aide to Secretary of War Henry Stimson, fielding issues related to black soldiers. The soldiers wrote: "We are treated like wild animals here, like we are inhuman. . . . Civilian polices have threatened to kill several soldiers. . . . Lieutenant Bromberg said all Negroes need to be beaten to death. . . . We never get enough to eat. In the hospital we are mistreated. Please help us." From Brackettville, Texas, another soldier wrote, "We're not even good as dogs, much less soldiers, even our General on the post hates the sight of a colored soldier."

These practices and attitudes inflicted damage in many ways. Walter Morris and his demoralized men were among those suffering.

Ashley Bryan drew this pen-and-ink sketch of two men in his company. Bryan captures their somber mood during a moment at rest.

An Inferiority Complex

Unlike many soldiers during World War II, Morris was not drafted into the Army. He was there by choice. He joined the Army in January 1940, just six months after graduating from high school. Three years later, he had come very close to his goal of becoming an officer. The review board suggested he join a service outfit and reapply in three months. Morris knew in his heart that he was a good leader.

He had also had his share of demeaning experiences and understood why it was sometimes, as he put it, "a natural thing for black soldiers to have an inferiority complex." He wanted to show his men how valuable they really were. He wanted to wipe out the idea that black men weren't smart enough or brave enough to jump out of airplanes. He wanted his soldiers to know that they were as up to the task as anyone else.

Watching the white students go through their routine, Morris had an idea. What if he had his men mimic the training of the white paratroopers? They could learn everything the paratroopers were learning, aside from jumping from the highest towers or out of airplanes—they would have needed official approval for that. But there was no reason they couldn't model themselves after the paratroopers. And if they *could* do what those paratroopers were doing, what might that do to boost their morale?

They Began to Act Like Soldiers

Morris put his plan into action one fall day in 1943.

"At four o'clock, when the white students left, we took over," Morris said with a glint in his eye.

He gathered the soldiers who weren't on guard duty that day. He marched them from the barracks out to the field. Double-time. He put them through their paces. Push-ups. Sit-ups. Jumping jacks. Running.

When the white students left, we took over.

They leaped off the five-foot platform to learn how to fall so the impact of a landing would be distributed evenly on the body. Otherwise, just the ankles or knees would take the brunt of the fall, which would lead to injuries.

After first going through the routine of hooking up their equipment and checking it, they lined up one by one to jump out of the stationary body of a C-47 cargo plane to simulate exiting an aircraft. Once they were out the door, the countdown to the chute opening began.

One thousand, two thousand, three thousand.

If a parachute doesn't open after three seconds, it is time to pull the reserve parachute. This was just a simulation on the ground, so the chutes did not actually open and a sawdust pit cushioned their fall.

"Within weeks, you could see the changes in our men: shoes shined, clothes pressed, hair cut and combed—morale was up," Morris said. "An amazing thing happened: they began to act like soldiers." The satisfaction in Morris's voice came through loud and clear.

Standing in the door of a C-47 mock-up, this trainee is about to take a practice jump into sawdust a few feet below him.

"When you talked to them, they looked you straight in the eye," he added. "They had found that, given the opportunity, they were just as good as the white students."

Morris wasn't the only one who noticed the changes going on. Someone high up had seen the black soldiers training in what was supposed to be an off-limits facility in the afternoons.

Morris got word to report to General Ridgely Gaither's office. Gaither was the commandant of The Parachute School. The eager young sergeant had no idea what was in store for him.

Morris's voice shook at the memory: "I was so nervous and afraid, I didn't even sleep that night."

During her visit to the Tuskegee Institute on March 29, 1941, and against the wishes of her escorts, Eleanor Roosevelt asked C. Alfred "Chief" Anderson to take her on a flight to show she trusted the skills of black pilots. Anderson, the first black pilot with a commercial license, and chief instructor of civilian pilots at Tuskegee, took her up for forty minutes.

CHAPTER THREE

I'M GOING TO TELL YOU A SECRET

The next morning, Morris rode his bike to the general's office. Had he done something wrong? Was he in trouble? He had taken it upon himself to completely restructure what his men were doing with their time — and had not asked anyone for permission. This was *not* the Army way.

"When I walked into the office, I was scared to death."

Morris was well aware of Gaither's reputation for being "tough as nails and just as straight."

"Explain to me what I saw," Gaither ordered.

Morris told Gaither about his men's morale problem and the scheme he had cooked up to fix it.

"It occurred to me that if I could get my men to go through that same calisthenics [exercises] as the white students, it might inspire them." As Morris spoke, he calmed down. He could tell from Gaither's reaction that the general was not angry.

In fact, he seemed impressed. Excited, even.

"Now," Gaither confided, "I'm going to tell you a secret — a top secret."

Ruby and Walter Morris

Gaither revealed that orders were on the way authorizing him to create a new, all-black unit of paratroopers: the 555th Parachute Infantry Company. He asked Morris to serve as first sergeant.

"You'll have black officers and black men," Gaither told Morris.

"It was such a shock to hear that—such a feeling—oh, my goodness." Morris was almost giddy at the remembrance. "My head was in the clouds. . . . My heart almost burst right there." He has told this next part of the story many times over, the significance of it never failing to make him chuckle. "I don't have any idea how I got [back] to my office. I don't know if I rode my bicycle or flew!"

There was something else Morris didn't know: his timing was perfect. Little by little, things had been happening behind the scenes to improve the status of blacks in the military. These changes had created the climate that led to Gaither's orders being possible. Morris had made his move in the right place at the right time.

A Great Many Improvements

Remember how Roosevelt's October 9, 1940, statement about the Selective Training and Service Bill did not satisfy enough of the requests made by black leaders? When that statement was released to the press—including the black newspapers—it upset a lot of people. With the presidential election coming up, the Democrats were worried that Roosevelt would lose the black vote. In part to make amends, in the weeks leading up to the election, the White House and the War Department announced that black aviation units would be formed, as well as new black combat units in the Army. Roosevelt promised that blacks would serve in all branches of the armed forces. A historic promotion was announced as well. Colonel Benjamin O. Davis Sr.—the highest-ranking black officer in the Army—was promoted to brigadier general, becoming the first African American to hold that title. The Republicans had already pointed out to black voters that one hundred white colonels had been promoted before Davis, so anyone paying attention to the news had a good understanding of the importance of this particular promotion.

Roosevelt promised that blacks would serve in all branches of the armed forces.

Brigadier General Davis conducted inspection tours of bases that trained African-American soldiers, investigating discrimination and advocating for better treatment when needed, both in the United States and overseas. He also served on the Advisory Committee on Negro Troop Policies. Davis urged the military to create more combat units and utilize black soldiers properly. When he discovered combat units that were continually passed over for overseas assignments, he put pressure on the War Department to send them.

The reason for the timing of Davis's promotion was the same as the one behind Roosevelt's appointment of the distinguished black scholar William Hastie to serve as Secretary of War Stimson's civilian aide. Stimson, who seemed to support segregation of the military, was annoyed by the appointment. He wrote in his diary, "The Negroes are taking advantage of this period just before the election to try to get everything they can in the way of recognition from the Army." In spite of Stimson's attitude and Hastie's realization that he "was not really welcomed by the military," over the next few years Hastie continued to try to persuade the War Department to improve conditions for African-American soldiers. He faced a lot of resistance but was proud of what was accomplished during his tenure, saying, "We were able to get significant numbers of black soldiers admitted to officers'

Some of Charles Alston's cartoons highlighted important black figures, such as this one of William Hastie, done in 1943.

candidate schools . . . who theretofore would have found their application for one reason or another, pigeonholed or rejected. . . . We were able to get a great many improvements in the conditions which blacks experienced on military bases."

They Should Be Given a Chance to Prove Their Mettle

First Lady Eleanor Roosevelt had also been making waves with her opinions about racial equality, both in civilian life and in the military. She was so outspoken that she became hated in the South. She asked the FBI to investigate whether it was true that black servants had formed "Eleanor Clubs" to fight for their rights. While the FBI did not discover any of these clubs, it did report that southerners thought of Eleanor as "the most dangerous individual in the United States today."

Southerners thought Eleanor Roosevelt was "the most dangerous individual in the United States."

It was partly due to Eleanor's close relationship with NAACP director Walter White that she pushed her husband about the Selective Training and Service Bill amendment requests. This in turn led to some of President Roosevelt's concessions after his October 9 press release. Secretary of War Stimson seemed to be just as irritated with Eleanor's efforts to improve conditions for African Americans as he was with Hastie's, implying that the president's actions were in part due to "Mrs. Roosevelt's intrusive and impulsive folly."

In addition to Eleanor's involvement with policies, she was a sympathetic ear for those who reached out to her. She received frequent letters from black soldiers alerting her to discrimination taking place on military bases.

Sergeant Henry Jones was one of many soldiers who wrote to Mrs. Roosevelt. He told her that the men in his unit were "loyal Americans . . . ready and willing to do their part . . . the fact that we want to do our best for our country and be valiant soldiers, seems to mean nothing to the Commanding Officer of our Post." Jones was writing on behalf of 121 other soldiers who signed the letter. "We do not ask for special privileges. . . . All we desire is to have equality; to be free to participate in all activities, means of transportation, privileges and amusements afforded any American soldier." Eleanor Roosevelt sent so many requests like this to Army Chief of Staff General George C. Marshall to investigate that Marshall had to assign two staff members just to answer them.

> *We do not ask for special privileges. . . . All we desire is to have equality.*

Eleanor made it her business to stay on top of the news affecting black soldiers. In 1943, when reports began to surface that black combat units weren't being sent to the front and that some of those units were being given service duties instead, she wrote to the War Department, saying they "should be given a chance to prove their mettle. I feel they have something to gain in the war."

Where Are Your Negro Paratroopers?

In keeping with Roosevelt's directive to form black aviation units, in July 1941, the Air Corps branch of the Army began training African-American pilots for the first time. That did not stop the chief of the Air Corps, General Henry "Hap" Arnold, from sending out a memo. It said that if the corps was forced to accept blacks, it would be limited to enlisted positions because he couldn't have black officers presiding over white enlisted men, as "this would create an impossible social problem." Regardless of Arnold's opinion, the nondiscrimination act was in place.

When Howard University law student Yancey Williams's application to be a pilot was ignored, he sued the War Department for violating the nondiscrimination act. The NAACP took up Williams's cause. Soon after the lawsuit was filed, FDR announced that the Tuskegee Institute in Alabama would host an aviation training program for black pilots.

A group of Tuskegee airmen in Ramitelli, Italy, March 1945. One of the only photos taken of them overseas by a professional photographer, this was shot by Toni Frissell, who was documenting war conditions in Europe for the U.S. government.

The 99th Pursuit Squadron—known as the Tuskegee Airmen—was the first group of black aviators to be trained. They proved to be exemplary pilots. Colonel Benjamin O. Davis Jr., son of Davis Sr., was among the first cadets and became their commander. Davis had applied to the Air Corps six years earlier but had been rejected then based on the explanation that "no black units were to be included."

Even having cleared this hurdle, the Tuskegee Airmen did not escape racism. They were kept apart from the white pilots, "white only" and "black only" signs went up on base, and the townspeople of Tuskegee, Alabama, treated them atrociously. Perhaps even harder to stand, almost 1,000 black pilots had been trained by the spring of 1943, but not one of them had been sent into combat.

Tuskegee pilot Louis Purnell wrote, "The Air Corps brass couldn't decide what to do with us so we flew and flew for nearly a whole year simply to maintain our proficiency." When that situation was finally rectified and the pilots were sent overseas on April 15, 1943—in part due to Eleanor Roosevelt's insistence—it was a major move forward. Colonel Davis said, "As we left the shores of the United States, we felt as if we were separating ourselves, at least for the moment, from the evils of racial discrimination."

The Tuskegee Airmen went on to achieve glory in World War II, flying more than 1,500 missions without ever losing one of their own to an enemy bomber, and earning a collective one hundred Distinguished Flying Crosses. What had started as an experiment to test whether black men were capable of handling aircraft—with some of the top brass in Stimson's War Department thinking they would fail—resulted in a spectacular success.

If the Air Corps could produce stellar black pilots, then why couldn't the Army produce stellar black paratroopers? That was the question that seemed to be on some people's minds. Bradley Biggs was the first officer accepted to the 555th. The story Biggs tells in a book he wrote about the Triple Nickles is that President Roosevelt visited The Parachute School in April 1943 (before Biggs arrived) and asked the commandant, "Where are your Negro paratroopers?" Over the years, different versions of this story have been told and retold. Some of the Triple Nickles men heard that it was Eleanor Roosevelt who had asked that probing question. Fort Benning's newspaper documents Roosevelt's 1943 visit there, putting him on the scene at the right time. Whether or not a Roosevelt actually did pose that question to the commandant, it certainly seemed to be a timely idea. And one thing is certain, as Morris says: "Blacks were asking, 'Why can't we have black paratroopers, too?'"

All of these things came into play the day General Gaither summoned Morris to his office. "He let me know that President Roosevelt had ordered General Marshall to form an all-black paratrooper unit," Morris said.

Benjamin O. Davis Jr., January 1942. Ten years earlier, when he was a cadet at West Point, no one would room with him and he ate alone. The leadership did nothing. Davis said, "It was designed to make me buckle, but I refused . . . I was not missing anything by not associating with them. They were missing a great deal by not knowing me."

Blacks were asking, "Why can't we have black paratroopers, too?"

The Trainasium, used during B Stage, is for agility exercises and tests a student's ability to carry out simple instructions and activities above ground level as well as conquer any fear of heights.

CHAPTER FOUR

I HAD A MISSION THAT WAS [ABOVE] AND BEYOND ME

Before the four-week paratrooper class began, Morris was given a little time off. He went home to share his proud news. "I showed off my boots—I had no business wearing them, but I had them." They were the tall, shiny, brown boots worn only by paratroopers.

Back at Fort Benning, training started in January 1944. Twenty black soldiers, including Morris, were about to go through the program. Morris, Clarence Beavers, and Elijah Wesby came out of Fort Benning. The other seventeen were recruited from the 92nd Infantry Division, stationed at Fort Huachuca, Arizona. These were tough guys who had already gone through infantry training.

The 92nd was historically an all-black unit—with white officers. Its roots can be traced back to the Buffalo Soldiers—African-American regiments in the Civil War. Historians generally agree that the nickname Buffalo Soldiers began on the western frontier, where these black soldiers' Cheyenne opponents were impressed with their fighting skills and thought their hair resembled that of the buffalo, which the Cheyenne held in high honor. The black soldiers accepted the nickname as a compliment. This early history has a direct connection to the 555th's nickname, the Triple Nickles. Since nickels had a buffalo on them for

Roger Walden

many years and most of the men came from the 92nd, "we became 'Triple Nickles' in honor of the Buffalo Soldiers," Morris recalled.

Roger Walden was one of the men from the 92nd. Like Morris, he had signed up for the Army voluntarily, but Walden was increasingly unhappy at Huachuca and eager to leave: "At Huachuca," he said, "it was obvious that very few black officers had command positions. . . . White officers who had goofed elsewhere were being sent [there]. . . . They had no compunction about letting it be known that they were being punished when sent to Huachuca. . . . I began to have misgivings about following this kind of officer into battle, and I became determined to get out." When the recruiters arrived to find good men for paratrooper training, Walden quickly volunteered.

The black officers who would be in charge of the 555th — three of whom also came from Fort Huachuca — went through the same training as the first group of twenty. Bradley Biggs was one of them. He was just twenty-two years old and had already served as a lieutenant in the 92nd Division. Biggs was so intent on making a good impression that he splurged for a taxi ride from the Columbus, Georgia, train station to Fort Benning instead of taking the chance that his pressed uniform would get wrinkled on the bus. The white cabdriver did not speak to him once during the forty-five-minute drive.

Bradley Biggs

Biggs met Morris his first morning at Fort Benning. Morris stood at attention and introduced himself.

"So here we stand," Biggs said to Morris. "You, the first Negro enlisted man accepted for the airborne forces, and me, the first officer."

They smiled at each other.

Biggs had grown up in one of the roughest neighborhoods in Newark, New Jersey, and was determined to do something of importance with his life. Being a part of the Triple Nickles offered him that opportunity. "We realized if we did it for ourselves, the rest would follow," he wrote. "We felt the pride of Negro America rested on our success. We were, in effect, on trial every day."

Our Lungs Begged for Air

Week one — or A Stage — was rough. "It was from daylight to dark, running, jumping, doing push-ups, getting our body in physical shape for the other three weeks of training," Morris remembered.

They ran several miles before breakfast, and that was just to warm up. They then maneuvered around obstacle courses, scaled walls, climbed ropes, learned hand-to-hand combat techniques, and ran some more. Even for men like Biggs, who had already trained as an infantry soldier and had played professional football for the all-black New York Brown Bombers, it was brutal. He recalled "running until our lungs begged for air and our boots felt like they were made of lead." It was the kind of training meant to push their limits — to see if they could stand it without collapsing or giving up.

One of the men, Carstell Stewart, who was already in top physical shape as a former track star and football player from Morgan State College, said, "They were trying to break us — that was a normal thing in that position. . . . It was a type of hazing situation: Are you tough enough? Can you compete? Can you be one of us? . . . It wasn't that they were white and we were black. It was just a one-on-one, man-to-man thing."

During A Stage, they were also taught about the equipment they would be using. There were lectures and demonstrations on how to handle parachutes on landings, how to keep from getting dragged, and how to keep themselves safe

June 1944. The second platoon of the 555th doing push-ups during A Stage.

Elijah Wesby has just jumped from the thirty-four-foot tower and his straps are still attached to the cable. Roger Walden assists in pulling Wesby down to unhook him. From the look of their clean uniforms and calm expressions, this appears to be a posed photo of their training.

during a jump. Mock jumps from the C-47 fuselage taught them how to exit an aircraft in the right position to avoid spinning when they fell, as well as how to position their bodies for landing. Learning how to hit the ground without injury is a key first step to becoming a paratrooper. What Morris's men had begun to learn while mimicking the white students was now a formal part of their training.

The Great Separator

During B Stage, the men began to practice operating their parachutes. The chutes used were modeled after the emergency parachutes pilots used to evacuate an aircraft in trouble. There was no quick release to detach the parachute from the harness after landing. Instead, you could either get up on your feet and run around your parachute—impossible in windy conditions—or lie down and pull one set of risers until the chute collapsed. It was tricky business, and important to shed the chute fast before it deflated to avoid being dragged by a gust of wind. Mastering how to unfasten the harness as swiftly as possible was crucial to success.

B Stage also brought the first real jump—from a height of thirty-four feet. This jump required them to put into practice the tight body position they had learned from the C-47 mock-door jumps and gave them a chance to maintain control on the way to the ground. No parachute opened on this jump; instead, the harness was hooked into a zip line. The thirty-four-foot tower was nicknamed the Great Separator because it separated those who had the courage and guts to go through with the jump from those who did not. Only one of the original twenty men couldn't bring himself to jump. The rest went right through the door.

The jump-sequence language that the men had already learned became very real at this point in their training. As each man took his place, he heard the instructor boom part of the same sequence (the full sequence wasn't needed because you can't sit down in the tower): "Stand in the door."

Then: "Go," and a slap on the leg. Most times, out they went. Sometimes an encouraging shove was needed. That was usually all it took, because each man, as Biggs observed, "knew that if he walked *down* those [tower] stairs, he walked away from his airborne career." That was the last thing any of them wanted.

Years later, Biggs described in his book what the jumps from the tower were like: "You would leave the mock tower placing both feet together, legs straight, head down with the chin on your chest, and both hands on the parachute counting, 'one thousand, two thousand, three thousand.'"

They all knew there were plenty of ways to get it wrong. Jumping with your eyes closed, called a blackout jump, and jumping with your hands grabbing for air or with your legs askew were just some examples of jumps that didn't receive a good mark—and several passing jumps were needed to move on to the next stage. Hubert Bridges was determined to get it right and asked two of his fellow Triple Nickles members—Leo Reed and McKinley Godfrey—to help him with some extra practice sessions late at night.

Hubert Bridges

C Stage raised the stakes even higher. The men moved on from the thirty-four-foot tower to ones that were 250 feet tall. The first jump from this height was from what was called a controlled descent tower. Although the parachute was attached to cables, there was still a dizzying view from the top of that tower. Here is how it worked: The first time down was on a two-man seat, to get used to the height. At the bottom, the seat was stopped before the riders reached the ground. The second time, a soldier was strapped into a harness, above which an attached parachute had already been opened. Then a cable would pull him straight up to the top of the tower. When it reached the top mark, a special hitch would release the jumper, who would then descend—slowed only by his parachute kept in line by cables. These preparatory runs give a jumper a sense of the height and the feeling of the chute taking him down before he is in charge of actually controlling the parachute himself.

The 250-foot "free tower," on the other hand, was a whole other experience. No gently guided ride there. Once the jumper and chute were raised to the hitch at the top of the tower and the chute was released, the jumper was in full control of the parachute. The instructor on the ground hollered out directions: "Keep your feet and knees together . . . elbows locked, go to the left," and so on. There were no cables to keep him from crashing into the tower if he failed to control his direction.

Sergeant Roger Walden was incredulous: "They looked to me like the Eiffel Tower. I thought, my God, what have I gotten into? I couldn't believe I'd go off one of those towers, yet I felt I had a mission that was [above] and beyond me, and I would give it all I had." That is exactly what he and the others did.

Then it was time for their final phase. D Stage. Jump Week.

Walter Morris gets his equipment checked before taking his first jump.

CHAPTER FIVE

BETS WERE MADE THAT BLACKS WOULD NEVER JUMP

The Triple Nickles were already beating the odds, already pushing the boundaries, but the reality of discrimination was never far enough away to be forgotten or ignored. African-American citizens and soldiers alike were still being kept out of "white" establishments, sectioned off into the back aisles of movie theaters, called vicious names, and targeted with unprovoked attacks. The irony of the bigger picture could not have been lost on anyone paying attention. "Soldiers were fighting the world's worst racist, Adolph Hitler, in the world's most segregated army," historian Stephen Ambrose later wrote.

Right in the heart of the nation's capital, one soldier reported a common occurrence: "While in uniform, I was not allowed to eat in white establishments. . . . It was not only insulting but hurtful because I was one of those fighting for the country." There were brutal results of prejudice as well. In January 1942, white military police in Alexandria, Louisiana, arrested and beat a black soldier. When black soldiers came to his defense and white civilians joined the side of the military police, the situation exploded into a full-scale riot.

In June 1943, on a hot day in a crowded park in Detroit, Michigan, fighting broke out among a few black and white people there. Tempers flared, and the violence spread like a virus as rumors of who had done what to whom incited rage in both blacks and whites in the vicinity. Windows were smashed, people were beaten, and by the next day, twenty-five black people and nine white people had been killed, and 1,000 more had been hurt.

Even as progress toward treating black citizens more fairly was being made—or perhaps *because* of it—clashes broke out. In May 1943, at the ADDSCO shipyard in Mobile, Alabama, a group of black welders had been promoted and were to work alongside white welders on the same job. One of the white welders wrote, "We don't any more want to work . . . alongside a Negro than you would want to take one into your dining room." When their joint shift was about to begin, the white welders arrived "armed with bricks, clubs, and bars, [and] attacked the Negro welders." The situation was resolved only when the company backed down and agreed to keep the black and white welders segregated.

Why Should We Be Treated as Second-Class Citizens?

At his own post, while training to be a paratrooper, Morris experienced the sting of seeing German and Italian prisoners of war buying cigarettes and candy at the post exchange. "Those men," he later recalled, "prisoners who killed American soldiers . . . [could] buy cigarettes or whatever they wanted to, but we . . . couldn't go into the post exchange." He also remembered watching the prisoners "sitting down at the same table with the white soldiers, drinking Cokes, and smoking, and having a good time. . . . We're in uniform, but we're not good enough to sit at the table with the prisoners of war!"

We're in uniform, but we're not good enough to sit at the table with the prisoners of war!

Ted "Tiger" Lowry was a 555th man with another impressive credit to his name in addition to being a paratrooper. He was a lightweight professional boxing champion who fought heavyweight champion Joe Louis while in the Army and went on to become the only person to last ten rounds with heavyweight champion Rocky Marciano—and did so twice—after the war. He was a fun-loving, outgoing guy, always smiling and a bit of a prankster. His wife, Alice, described him as "a man who never met a stranger." Lowry had his own vivid recollection of prejudice during the war.

One day, he stepped onto a bus. His U.S. Army dress uniform was crisp, his pants creased, his brown boots polished to a shine. Pinned to his jacket were the kind of silver wings that signify only one thing: paratrooper. But this accomplished soldier couldn't occupy any of the first open seats in the front of the bus.

He walked past the two front rows as the white soldiers sitting there laughed and pointed. He ignored their taunts. He knew better than to risk everything he was working toward. He held his temper and walked to the back of the bus.

From his seat, his eyes traveled up the length of the bus, up to the front. They settled on some of the men who laughed. That's when he saw it: three simple letters stamped on the backs of their jackets.

Ted "Tiger" Lowry

POW.

Prisoner of war.

Lowry was from the North, born in New Haven, Connecticut, and raised in Portland, Maine. This kind of racism was new to him. "There, in the South," he said, "I found out that I was black." It was bad enough that the black soldiers had to suffer this treatment from the white American soldiers, but to have to take a backseat to the POWs was even worse.

Bradley Biggs's cool-tempered demeanor changed when he reflected on the prisoners of war the 555th encountered. "That irked us no end," Biggs said, frowning. There was pain and anger in his voice. "That hurt the living blazes out of us. Why should we be treated as second-class citizens when . . . prisoners of war can come here and get service and treatment that we're denied?"

These trailblazing black paratrooper students were completely segregated from the white students on their post. As Morris put it, "We were in one section of Fort Benning, and they were in another. . . . We had nothing to do with the white soldiers; they had nothing to do with us."

Clarence Beavers has a sharp memory and has given many interviews about being in the Triple Nickles. "We trained, ate, were housed, and made our five jumps as a separate unit," he said. "We had four white training instructors who had volunteered for the job. While other trainees came through the front door and went to [the] counter for their food, we had to come in by the side door and go right to the first table on our left. We were not allowed to go to the counter." The irritation in his voice was clear. "They didn't want us to stand on line with the white trainees, so they had someone bring us our food."

Our Rifles Were Empty

There were other mistreatments. The Triple Nickles were barred from the post's main theater, a principal source of entertainment. "We had no recreation over there whatsoever," Clarence Beavers recalled. The men also found their housing unacceptable. "We were put in a hut," Beavers said with audible disdain, "with twenty of us, double-bunked, it really should have held no more than fifteen men at the most, but . . . being black, we were put in there separate from all the others. It was heated by one potbellied stove in the dead of winter."

Even though the military was allowing the Triple Nickles to become paratroopers, discrimination practices affected their training. They were not, for example, allowed access to ammunition. "Our rifles were empty," Morris told a radio interviewer. When asked why that was, you could almost hear Morris shaking his head: "I have no idea, other than the fact that the Army did not trust the black soldiers to handle munitions because he didn't have the intelligence. . . . They thought we might have shot ourselves in the foot by mistake."

Jesse Mayes, who came to the 555th wearing his polished brass second lieutenant wings with honor in 1945, had previous experiences with discrimination in the Army. "I remember when I applied for OCS [Officer Candidate School]. My commanding officer . . . said, 'I'm not about to send you to OCS. Smartest Negro I know is on my farm in Mississippi.' Now, sure, I wanted to slug him in

This is the area at Fort Benning where the Triple Nickles put on their parachutes and loaded the planes.

the mouth. . . . It would have got me a court-martial. That guy would have won. So you learn. You learn by what my granddaddy called stooping to conquer."

Like Lowry and Biggs, Carstell Stewart was raised in the North and was not accustomed to living with southern racist attitudes. Wincing, he said, "You could cut prejudice, you could see it . . . you could smell it." He had a particularly ugly experience in a store in Columbus, Georgia, where he was taunted and threatened with a gun if he didn't do as he was told. Stewart told himself, "Be cool and get through it and move on." He said, "[I] swallowed my pride because I knew what I was there for. They thought we were going to be failures. . . . That's what they wanted to do, to cause problems, to make us not be able to bring about a successful conclusion, being a black parachute group. . . . We had boots and they figured we shouldn't be wearing boots."

Jesse Mayes

Some of the white soldiers even doubted that the 555th was going to make the cut. Morris said, "Both officers and enlisted were making bets that we wouldn't jump—we'd be too afraid. The thing that inspired us was that . . . it was an opportunity for black troops to enter something they could be proud of." Intelligent and well spoken, Walden confirmed Morris's view: "The general feeling on base was that African Americans simply were not good enough to be paratroopers. At the time, bets were made that blacks would never jump."

In his book about the Triple Nickles, Biggs talked about encountering both prejudice and acceptance as a paratrooper. Some of the positive interactions may be attributed to his officer status, as well as to the attitude he knew he had to maintain to succeed. He wrote that although his training instructors were white and some were from the South, "because of the camaraderie of the airborne club, or out of respect, or simply because they were professionals, we sensed no racial undertones in their attitudes or actions, no resentment that men of a different color were now entering their special world." He also noted that after graduation, the Triple Nickles officers "would often go to [the] theater with the

Bradley Biggs

white officers who had been their instructors. Once we had earned our wings, something of a brotherhood developed. . . . This relative racial calm upset the racists on the post."

About the racism they did encounter, the always polished and professional Biggs wrote, "We were determined . . . to concentrate on our main mission. Always on our minds was the thought that, if we failed, the arrogant aristocrats at the Army's helm would have the excuse to say, 'See? We gave them a chance and they couldn't handle it.'" His outlook came from personal experience.

A year earlier, a white officer had given Biggs an order that he felt was unfair. Biggs was outspoken to his superiors about the incident, and his resistance was labeled insubordination, for which he had to endure court-martial charges. Biggs met face-to-face with Benjamin O. Davis Sr., who lectured him on how to better handle prejudice.

"If you learn to keep your mouth shut and your eyes open, you'll go far in the Army and I will tell you why." Davis proceeded to tell Biggs that there were going to be openings for more black tankers, pilots, and even paratroopers. "When he said paratroopers, that sparked my ears." Biggs's voice lit up with excitement.

Davis told Biggs, "Curb your tongue" and "quiet your temper. . . . Your anger will ruin your hopes for a military career," he scolded. "More opportunities will come to our soldiers but we must be ready for them."

These types of experiences—being coached by superiors like Davis, coping with the bets that they wouldn't jump, being kept out of restaurants and movie theaters—brought home the knowledge that the 555th had a double burden to shoulder. They had to prove to the world that they had the bravery and skill it took to succeed, *and* they had to do it while not reacting to the prejudice they ran into around every corner. But Biggs and company were stoic. "We fought segregation and discrimination and intolerance. They tried to burn us out. . . . It made us stronger. It made us angry. It made us persevere."

Bets or no bets, the Triple Nickles did persevere. They were ready for Jump Week.

They tried to burn us out. . . . It made us stronger.

D Stage Was the Real Thing

This was it. No turning back. "D Stage was the real thing," Biggs wrote. It was time to move beyond the towers and jump out of airplanes. Become *airborne*.

Before that could happen, the Triple Nickles had to finish learning how to pack parachutes (some of which was taught in A Stage) and review everything they had learned up to this point. There is no room for error at this stage of paratrooper training. Error can result in death: "a tangled mess of bones and flesh that had to be dug out of the ground."

Everywhere they went, they practiced their techniques. Stepping off a curb? They stepped off with the correct form as if they were jumping—"heels together, knees slightly bent, hands folded across his chest, counting 'one thousand, two thousand, three thousand.'" Leaving a room as a group? They went in stick formation—a line of paratroopers one after the other, as if they were exiting a plane. Every routine had to be so much a part of them that it was second nature.

And then it was time.

Fear was not shameful. It was part of the process. Normal. If you didn't have a healthy respect for the danger, you were a fool. The men dealt with the fear through humor, sometimes making jokes about staying behind.

Samuel Robinson

He Was the First Man to Integrate the Army!

"I remember every second of my first jump," Morris said. The memories stayed fresh for Samuel Robinson, too. Eyes twinkling, he seemed to be right back in the moment: "I guess I was doing a little praying when I come out and count that one thousand, two thousand, three thousand, and the chute would open at two and a half seconds, and then I would get relieved." He said the last part with a grin.

Clarence Beavers reflected on the moments just after a jump. Pensive, he said that there is "a lot of enjoyment in the ride. . . . It's that still quiet."

When the officers took their first jump, the mood was serious. "I slept very little the night before our first jump. . . . The usual banter was missing. Each of us knew that we were about to do something no other black officers in military history had ever done before," Biggs said.

Each of the two groups going through training—the twenty enlisted men and the six officers who followed just after them—had to complete four daylight jumps and one night jump in order to earn their wings.

That first jump into the dark black night, counting on their skills, their instincts, their guts, is the turning point for paratroopers. Once that was under their belts, they knew they had what it took. "It was the moment of real truth," Biggs wrote.

During their third jump, a distinguished guest visited. General Davis wanted to see how they were doing. He was flown in a spotter plane to watch them jump. After the men were back on the ground, Davis approached Beavers.

"What is the minimum size parachute unit the War Department contemplates using in combat?"

The original test platoon riding high in a C-47 transport plane as they prepare to make one of their required five qualifying jumps. The first four men (right to left) are Calvin Beal, Clarence Beavers, Ned Bess, and James Kornegay.

Test platoon member Lonnie Duke shown just after landing from a jump at Fort Benning.

Beavers responded that he believed it was a battalion—300 to 1,000 soldiers.

"Then why are you training a cadre for a company-size unit of black parachutists?" Davis asked. (A company is made up of 62 to 190 soldiers.)

Beavers replied, "That is all the War Department sent us."

It is likely that this interaction helped the 555th receive their orders just a month later: to increase their size from a company to a battalion.

Only three of the twenty men from the test platoon failed to graduate—Cleo Washington, James S. Williams, and Emerald Jones. Jones was out when he wouldn't jump from the thirty-four-foot tower, but he was well liked and stayed on as the company cook.

On February 18, 1944, sixteen soldiers made history by becoming the first African-American paratroopers.

The seventeenth man, Carstell Stewart, had to interrupt his training when his mother died but quickly returned to finish his course. It was harder for Stewart without his buddies. He had to train with the white students, who,

Graduation photo of the first black paratroopers. Front row, left to right: Walter Morris, Jack Tillis, Leo Reed, Daniel Weil, Hubert Bridges, Alvin Moon, Ned Bess, and Roger Walden. Back row, left to right: McKinley Godfrey Jr., Elijah Wesby, Samuel Robinson, Calvin Beal, Robert Greene, Lonnie Duke, Clarence Beavers, and James Kornegay. Not pictured is Carstell Stewart, who graduated a week later.

Robinson attested with a look of sadness, "were really down on him." In a very matter-of-fact way that indicated he had come to terms with the situation, Stewart said, "You know what they think about you. They really don't like you, they don't want you." He said this next part with some punch, emphasizing each and every word: "But you've got to stay in and hang." Just because he understood how things were didn't mean Stewart didn't feel some resentment. You could hear it in his voice when he added, "In that situation, nobody wanted to help me pack a chute, nobody wanted to . . . cooperate with me, so I had to pack my own chute. . . . I didn't have anybody to lean on. . . . I had nobody to talk to. I was out there by myself."

Decades later, Walden reflected on Stewart's situation. With a sympathetic tone, he acknowledged, "It was rougher for him probably than those of us that were all together, because we could talk about things at night in the barracks, and we would encourage each other." Morris noted, "Technically he was the first man to integrate the Army!" Carstell's wings were pinned on his chest just a week after the others.

A Smoothly Running, Highly Skilled Combat Company

On March 4, the six officers completed jump school and received their wings. Even in the middle of this positive and exciting event, there was still an undercurrent of prejudice the men couldn't shake.

"When we got our wings," Biggs said, "we went off to Main Post, and I asked for membership in the Officers' Club. They said, 'No, we are going to give you your own club.' What they did was convert a service area . . . gave us a cook, and called it an officers' club. It was insulting. . . . We were part of the Army's elite troops. We completed some of the Army's most intense and demanding training . . . so why should we be treated as second-class citizens?"

The first six officers graduated on March 4, 1944. They are, left to right: Jasper Ross, Clifford Allen, Bradley Biggs, Edwin Wills, Warren "Cal" Cornelius, and Edward Baker.

With the officers on board, the 555th was now the first all-black paratrooper unit in the U.S. Army. The Army let it be known that it wanted more volunteers. "We got applications from everywhere," Morris said. As before, soldiers who got word of the opportunity were eager to make a difference. Carl Reeves was a mess steward when he found out about the 555th. "This was a chance for me, really, to prove that I could do something besides serve food to cadets."

For the second time, Morris was summoned to General Gaither's office. This time, he wasn't worried.

Morris has a knack for infusing his sense of humor into a serious story. "He was serving as my godfather," Morris jested, chuckling for a second. "And he said, Morris, I want you to go back to OCS [Officer Candidate School]. This is going to be a battalion. . . . They're going to need more officers."

The platoon did expand, adding new recruits who needed to be trained. Meanwhile, the first twenty-three men embarked on specialized training for combat. The men assumed they were headed for battle. Morris said, "We started combat training preparing troops to go overseas." As Beavers remembered, that included "how to . . . shoot under combat, how to respond to enemy attack, how to . . . fight as a squad in enemy territory . . . and how to assemble and fight as a company." They also learned to be jumpmasters, parachute riggers, pathfinders, and communications experts.

This still from a video shows the 555th carefully checking their chutes before a jump.

In stick formation, members of the 555th are inspected before boarding a jump plane.

In April 1944, General Gaither took the 555th's combat training even further by putting them through four weeks of Advanced Tactical Division (ATD). They were taught individual survival skills as well as skills to support one another as a team in combat. These included judo, hand-to-hand combat, machine-gun operation, and rapid-fire shooting with rifles. During their continued jump training, each paratrooper had the chance to command the squad. It was training that, Biggs said, "molded us into a smoothly running and highly skilled combat company."

"By the time we left," he said, "we had a company of leaders as well as a fine-tuned combat unit." This specialized training also reinforced the idea that they would be headed for combat. "Upon completing that," Beavers said, "we felt we had met everything the Army wanted and were now ready to go overseas."

By mid-July 1944, the 555th had been moved to Camp Mackall, North Carolina. They were 165 strong, with eleven officers. In November, the company was redesignated the 555th Parachute Infantry Battalion. More men were added and trained until the battalion had more than four hundred men. Among them were Melvin Lester, John Mills, and Carl Reeves. Ted Lowry, the strong, stocky paratrooper who suffered in silence the day those German POWs laughed at him on that Georgia bus, had also joined the group.

The Triple Nickles had earned their right to fight. But would they be given the chance?

Taken in March 1945, this photograph captures the feelings of soldiers William E. Thomas and Joseph Jackson with an artillery shell labeled "Happy Easter Adolph" and the extra shells cradled in an "Easter basket."

CHAPTER SIX

WE WERE GOING TO TANGLE WITH HITLER

Tuskegee Airman Luther H. Smith was in a German prison camp after being captured when his plane crashed. A German officer confronted Smith. "With utter contempt he said, 'You volunteered to fight for a country that lynches your people.'"

"You might as well have hit me with a heavy stick," Smith said. The next day, when the officer launched at him again, Smith had his comeback ready: "You people are just as bad. . . . Your German Jews, you lynch them. . . . I am black American. It is my home. I will fight for it because I have no other home, and by fighting for it, I can make America better."

Despite all the racial problems and prejudices the Triple Nickles experienced—both on and off military posts—they were still as eager as ever to head overseas into battle. They were not alone in this sentiment.

The United States had joined forces to fight a war in which freedom was at stake. Germany's Nazi Party, led by Adolf Hitler, was carrying out the worst hate crimes the world had ever seen. African-American journalist J. Saunders Redding wrote that blacks "in America know a lot about freedom and love it more than a great many people who have long had it. . . . This is a war to keep

Famous boxing champion and WWII soldier Joe Louis fought 555th member Ted Lowry.

me free." Joe Louis, the famous heavyweight champion boxer who served as a private in the Army during World War II, had his own thoughts about why black men volunteered to help fight: "There may be a whole lot wrong with America, but there's nothing that Hitler can fix."

There were also, of course, African Americans who became too angry or resentful to want to serve. Harvard graduate and history professor John Hope Franklin was just one example. He volunteered for the Navy and was rejected because of his color. "If I was able—physically, mentally, every other kind of way, able and willing to serve my country— and my country turned me down on the basis of color, then my country did not deserve me." Other soldiers joined out of a sense of patriotism but were treated so badly that they lost their feeling of belonging to America. Private Bert Babero wrote, "I didn't hesitate to come when I believed I was needed. . . . I honestly believed that . . . I comprised an important part of this nation and it was my patriotic duty. . . . My attitude now is greatly changed."

And yet there were thousands who were passionate about defending their nation regardless of their status in American society—or in fact, in part *because* of their status. In addition to patriotism, a sense of adventure, and a chance for steady work—the same appeal the war held for many white soldiers—an underlying factor was the hope that their contribution to the war effort and their loyalty to the nation would be rewarded with better treatment after the war. This soldier's feelings were echoed by many: "I just thought . . . when we got back home they would have to recognize us . . . and say 'These people are A-number-one, so we'll have

If my country turned me down on the basis of color, then my country did not deserve me.

to treat them as citizens.'" Another said, "I have to go. . . . Part of it is so I can say, 'This is my country. I fought for it and you can't deny me.'"

I have to go. . . . Part of it is so I can say, "This is my country. I fought for it and you can't deny me."

These men believed fighting for their country was a way to show loyalty and achieve the right to full citizenship, which was exactly the message that many of the black newspapers sent to their readership. Others disagreed, questioning why anyone without full rights would ever want to put his life on the line. One direct response to this was the creation of the Double V Campaign, with its slogan "Victory at Home and Victory Abroad."

This 1943 Charles Alston cartoon was part of the Double V Campaign to convince blacks that by serving their nation during wartime they would also be taking strides toward triumphing against racism on the home front.

The Parachute Jump . . . Only a Means to an End

Paratrooper training is all about being combat ready. Biggs, itching to prove that the 555th had what it took, described the connection between training and combat: "Detailed and carefully rehearsed as it was, the parachute jump was still only a means to an end: the capture of an enemy ground position, a bridge, a road junction, an airfield, or a communications center." The Triple Nickles were most definitely ready, confirmed by an inspection by General Ben Lear, whose opinion carried a lot of weight. During his time with the 555th, he told them

This group shot includes (front row, left to right): Edwin Wills, Richard Williams, Bradley Biggs, and Roger Walden. In the middle of the back row is Harry Sutton. The other paratroopers are unidentified.

they were "one of the finest group of soldiers I have ever seen."

The timing of their readiness was superb. At least that's what the Triple Nickles thought.

It was now the end of December 1944. While all this training was taking place for soldiers around the country, the war was raging overseas. Six months earlier, Great Britain and the United States had launched the most massive amphibious assault ever. About 5,000 ships traveled across the English Channel, carrying more than 150,000 men and 30,000 vehicles to the coast of France. From the air, more than 13,000 paratroopers dropped behind enemy lines. The Allies liberated French villages from the Germans and took back Paris. They were winning the war. But on December 16, 1944, the Germans launched a surprise counterattack of 250,000 men that cut a path more than eighty miles wide into the Allied lines.

Tank driver Claude Mann of the 761st near Nancy, France, November 1944

The U.S. fought back with more than a half million men—including the all-black 761st Tank Battalion, which fought under General George S. Patton. Like the Tuskegee Airmen and the Triple Nickles, the 761st was created as an "experimental" specialty unit.

Huge numbers of replacement soldiers were needed. General Dwight D. Eisenhower, the Allies' supreme commander, put out a call for urgent help. Lieutenant General John Lee wrote the appeal after consulting with Eisenhower and General Davis, who was now working under Lee. Lee's letter invited black soldiers with infantry training to volunteer for "the privilege of joining our veteran units at the front to deliver the knockout blow." It also stated that black soldiers would be allowed "the opportunity of fighting shoulder to shoulder" with white soldiers and promised black soldiers an assignment "without regard to color or race to the units where assistance is most needed." The letter went so far as to say that black soldiers would "share the glory of victory," something black leaders had been asking for throughout the war.

By the time the black soldiers were sent to the front lines, however, Eisenhower had gotten push-back from other generals, so he recalled Lee's letter and replaced it with a modified version. Instead of putting white and black soldiers directly together, smaller all-black platoons were integrated into white units. As a result, some living and recreation facilities *were* integrated. It was a big step forward, even though it included a step back. Perhaps most significant, the experience changed the minds of some white soldiers. The following story from the famed Battle of the Bulge—which likely represents other similar stories— illuminates how.

On March 13, 1945, a company from the 99th Infantry Division was in serious trouble. The Germans surrounded them. Casualties were high. The number

Just inland from Omaha Beach in France after the D-Day invasion, an African-American platoon gets ready to eliminate a German sniper holding up an advance.

of living dropped every hour. The wounded—including their commander—lay bleeding, unable to be evacuated. Ceaseless gunfire had trapped them all. Then, in the distance, the company heard men coming. Cautiously they looked and listened for signs that the approaching men were American and not the enemy. But even when they saw the telltale American uniforms, the faces they saw confused them for a moment. Only two were white. The reaction that came next stuck in the mind of one of the black soldiers walking toward them, Harold Robinson: "They were all southern boys, but they sure were glad to see us." Although the trapped

> **They were all southern boys, but they sure were glad to see us.**

white soldiers couldn't risk giving their exact location away by shouting, they couldn't contain themselves completely. They cheered and waved anyway, as quietly as they could.

As David P. Colley writes in *Blood for Dignity*, his book about the black soldiers who fought at the Bulge, the trapped soldiers were "seeing something American soldiers had not seen for more than 150 years. . . . The last time blacks had served shoulder to shoulder with whites in infantry units was in Washington's Continental Army." In the end, the directives issued first by Lee and then by Eisenhower were, after all, just words on a page. The reality of the battlefront was something else entirely. When the bullets were flying and white soldiers needed backup, it didn't matter one bit what color their replacements were or how close together on the field they stood.

A white southern sergeant from a different unit later spoke about the profound effect the integration experiment during the Battle of the Bulge had on him: "I said I'd be damned if I'd wear the same patch they did. After that first day, when we saw how they fought, I changed my mind. They're just like any of the other boys to us." In fact, opinion surveys given by the Army Research Branch (ARB) showed that before the Battle of the Bulge, only 33 percent of white soldiers had a positive response to including blacks in their companies. Afterward, a whopping 77 percent felt favorably about the idea. Brigadier General Davis said that the decision to integrate in the Battle of the Bulge was "the greatest since enactment of the Constitutional amendments following the

LEFT OUT, BUT NOT FORGOTTEN

MANY PHOTOGRAPHS showing black units were left out of the record and, like these, were not shown until decades after the war. In 2009, William G. Dabney, the last known survivor of the 320th Antiaircraft Barrage Balloon Battalion, traveled to France for the 65th anniversary of the D-Day invasion. He said, "It makes you feel bad, when you don't get the recognition like the white soldiers, that they threw your name in the garbage." Another D-Day veteran, Paul Parks, recalls, "They didn't film us. They didn't interview us."

Above: Lieutenant General George Patton awards the Silver Star to Private Ernest A. Jenkins. October 1944.

Right: Members of the 761st Tank Battalion check equipment before leaving for combat. September 27, 1944.

Former corporal Charles Sprowl of the 490th Port Battalion, now 90, asks, "Where were we in *The Longest Day* or *Saving Private Ryan*?" referring to two famous films about D-Day. "Where were we in the history books?"

About the Battle of the Bulge, 761st Tank Battalion Private Floyd Dade remembers, "We had to prove to the world and our own people that we could fight. They even said we couldn't even operate the mechanized equipment. But we were the best."

Above: Members of the 92nd Division pass ammunition near Massa, Italy. November 1944.

Left: The USS *Mason* was the first Navy ship to have a largely African-American crew. March 29, 1944.

Below: Marines during the Battle of Peleliu in the Pacific. September 15, 1944.

Efforts are ongoing to recognize and honor some of the black veterans who have gone unnoticed. Historians and scholars are still looking for photographs and other artifacts that can document missing history and help make up for lost time.

emancipation [of slaves]." He wanted the ARB's opinion surveys made public to prove that integration would not cause mass disruption, but those who favored military segregation—including Army Chief of Staff General George C. Marshall and Secretary of War Henry Stimson—said no. Marshall argued that "the conditions under which the platoons were organized were most unusual" during that time, and therefore were not a good measure of success.

> **The Triple Nickles had good reason to believe it was finally their time to go.**

Because of all of this, as well as the fact that the 82nd Airborne and the 101st Airborne had lost a lot of men and that the 555th was ready for combat, the Triple Nickles had good reason to believe it was finally their time to go. Biggs's comment summed up their feelings: "At last, we thought, we were going to tangle with Hitler."

A Highly Classified Mission

Their orders never came.

In fact, as soon as the Battle of the Bulge was over, so were the military's moves toward integration. The black soldiers were sent back to their previous assignments, many of which were labor assignments. Photographers and reporters documenting the war—accidentally or purposely, or some of each—did not include the black soldiers' participation on the battlefields. Some of the units were even overlooked for recognition for their service—another step backward after the promise of sharing "the glory of victory." The performance of the 761st Tank Battalion during the Battle of the Bulge, for example, had led Major General E. H. Hughes to recommend them for a Distinguished Unit Citation. Citations were given to twelve of the white units that had fought with the 761st, but Eisenhower would not sign the citation for the black unit.

Instead of facing Hitler, the 555th was given yet another round of specialized training. Even though men were needed overseas, somehow the black soldiers did not seem to be needed quite as much. While white soldiers trained and were shipped overseas, black soldiers trained—and then trained some more. This happened with the 92nd and 93rd Infantry Divisions, too, although both eventually saw some combat.

Instead of being part of the replacements after the Battle of the Bulge, the Triple Nickles continued to be fine-tuned into elite paratrooper fighting machines.

Finally, in April 1945, an order was sent. By this time, though, the war in Europe was winding down. Biggs later assessed the situation: although morale was high and they were ready, "the German armies were collapsing. . . . The fall of the German capital was only weeks away. It seemed unlikely that any more paratroopers would be needed."

So where were they going?

To Pendleton Air Base in Pendleton, Oregon, for what their orders called a "highly classified" mission.

The Triple Nickles left Camp Mackall on May 5, 1945. As they made their way west on a train trip that took six days, there was much conversation among the men. Some wondered what they would do in Pendleton. Others thought they were getting ready to ship to the Pacific to fight the Japanese, where the war was still going strong. Morris was one of them.

> *We assumed we were going to join General MacArthur in the Pacific theater.*

He was humble but confident. "We assumed we were going to join General MacArthur in the Pacific theater," he said. "We were so happy."

The train clattered across the countryside. As they got close, they stopped for supplies and fuel. Morris and some of the men walked to a general store. A few white loggers were sitting around a potbellied stove, chatting.

"Well, you got here at last," one of them said.

Morris responded, "You were expecting us?"

"Oh, yeah, you colored soldiers, paratroopers, are going to fight forest fires for us. You're going to be smokejumpers."

"How do you know?" Morris asked.

"Well, we read it in the *New York Times*."

Loadmasters from the 555th heave heavy smokejumping gear into a C-47 in Pendleton, Oregon.

CHAPTER SEVEN

WE WERE SOLDIERS.
WE DID WHAT WE HAD TO DO.

"We had no idea what smokejumpers were," Morris said. "It was a letdown, really, because we thought we were going to fight the enemy."

The paratroopers soon learned that smokejumpers are firefighters who parachute down into fires in remote areas. It is an effective way to reach forest fires—much faster than on foot or on mules—and was a fairly new practice. The Forest Service had been doing it only since 1939.

The Triple Nickles received their orders in Pendleton, and some would argue that they *were* about to fight the enemy—just not where or how they had ever imagined. It wasn't merely a heavy lightning season or careless campers that caused the Forest Service to need extra men that spring. It was the Japanese.

More than three years earlier, on December 7, 1941, Japan had bombed Pearl Harbor, Hawaii. Japan's goal had been to destroy the American naval ships stationed there, thus preventing the U.S. from interfering in the war. The Pearl Harbor attack had sunk four battleships, destroyed 188 aircraft, and killed more than 2,400 Americans. But the Japanese plan backfired. Instead of keeping America out of the war, Pearl Harbor triggered the moment America entered World War II. It also marked the beginning of a growing fear and hatred between the United States and Japan that would take decades to heal.

We Can Fight and Die Just As Well As Any Other American

Yuzuru "John" Takeshita was born in America. He lived in California and was just fifteen years old when Pearl Harbor was bombed. Yet suddenly his own neighbors considered him a threat.

"My teacher asked us [Japanese Americans] who were Boy Scouts to turn in our knives and compasses and flashlights. . . . I suppose she feared that we might use them for sabotage . . . that we might be waiting for the right moment." He said this with a nervous laugh. "It was a very scary, uncertain time."

Takeshita was just one of thousands of Japanese Americans who, overnight, were seen as the enemy in their own country. People lost their businesses and were fired from their jobs. One young man had done yard work for a neighbor who had always been friendly, but when he showed up after Pearl Harbor, she told him to go home. During the Pearl Harbor attack, a Japanese-American soldier who happened to be out of uniform was almost killed by a fellow American soldier who assumed he was the enemy. Two high-school football players in California were harassed by their teammates, and when they stuck up for themselves, the principal kicked them out of school. Most Japanese Americans didn't know where Pearl Harbor was. They had never even heard of it.

Just the same, as Tom Kawagushi recalled, "I had the strangest feeling that all the eyes were on me." He and his brother decided "there's only one thing we can do—enlist. After all, you and I are Americans." But when they went to the recruiting office, "they threw us out. They said, 'We don't want any Japs around here.' And I cried." Sumi Seki's memory of the time perfectly captured what was going on: "We had the face of the enemy."

We had the face of the enemy.

With a nation now fearing this enemy, panic won and the unthinkable happened. President Franklin D. Roosevelt issued Executive Order 9066, which resulted in more than 120,000 "people of Japanese ancestry" being rounded up and put in internment camps. Over half of them were children. People lost their homes, their businesses. Families were split up. It made no difference whether they were born and raised in America. They looked Japanese. They looked like the enemy. And so they were treated as the enemy—even though that treatment violated their rights as American citizens.

April 5, 1942. People of Japanese ancestry arrive at the Santa Anita Assembly Center from San Pedro, California. From there, they were moved to relocation centers.

Famous photographer Ansel Adams shot this street scene at the Manzanar Relocation Center in California, showing rows of internment camp houses. People lost their homes and businesses and were forced to live here.

Japanese Americans and African Americans had more in common during the war than they might have known. At a time when their nation treated both minorities badly, for many, their patriotism moved them to rise above it. Remarkably, from within the barracks of the internment camps, many Japanese Americans volunteered for the military and were accepted (unlike Kawagushi). One soldier, who served with the 442nd Regimental Combat Team—an all-Japanese-American unit that earned the most medals of *any* World War II unit—had this to say: "We had a mission and that mission was to show them that we can fight and die just as well as any other American." Another said, "A lot of us felt that this was our only chance to demonstrate our loyalty. We would never get a second chance. This was it."

This passion to prove their loyalty and worth was something the Triple Nickles felt in their bones. So despite the twinge of disappointment they felt, they accepted their secret mission in Pendleton with dedication and commitment. They weren't being sent overseas to fight the war, but they were being sent to fight a threat by the Japanese on American soil. Code name: Operation Firefly.

One of the Best-Kept Secrets of World War II

The very same day the Triple Nickles had boarded their train to Pendleton, a tragedy was unfolding near their destination. It was a sunny spring morning in Bly, Oregon, on May 5, 1945. A young pastor and his wife, Archie and Elsye Mitchell, were getting ready to take a group of five young teenage Sunday-school students for an afternoon of fishing and picnicking. Elsye baked a chocolate cake to take along with their lunch, and Archie gathered the fishing gear. Once the car was packed, the Mitchells and their five passengers headed for Leonard Creek.

As they neared the fishing spot, they saw a truck stuck in the mud. The men from the truck told Archie that the road was not passable, so they should park nearby and hike the rest of the way to the creek. Elsye and the kids got out and started walking. As Archie was parking the car, his wife called out to him, "Look what I found, dear."

Something made Archie bolt into the woods, calling, "Don't touch it, don't touch it!" But it was too late.

Elsye and all five teenagers were killed by the blast.

What exactly had Elsye discovered in those woods?

Immediately following the explosion, a rescue team, a sheriff, and the Army were called to the scene. The military personnel found a large deflated balloon, debris from a bomb that had exploded, and four more bombs that had not gone off.

Back in Bly, it was obvious that something had gone terribly wrong as men in uniform trod in and out of the woods. Rumors began to swirl. Family members of the victims were contacted and sworn to secrecy. Eva Fowler, Elsye's sister, said, "We were all told not to talk about this over the phone. It was not to be put in the newspapers, or on the radio, or anything."

At a press conference the next day, officials reported the loss of the only Americans to die as a direct action of the enemy in the continental United States during World War II. The official word was that it was "an explosion of unknown origin." But the military knew exactly what it was. It was one of the best-kept secrets of World War II.

Don't Think Too Much About It

It had all started five months after Japan attacked Pearl Harbor, when America retaliated. The retaliation took the form of the Doolittle Raid, an attack on Tokyo by air, which sent a clear message to the Japanese that they were vulnerable at home.

Japan, in turn, was determined to instill fear in the American people, to make them realize that they, too, could be attacked within their own borders. The Japanese set out to invent a weapon that would be able to reach the continental United States.

They succeeded.

Their clever invention began with their discovery of the narrow and powerful air currents we now know as the jet stream. The Japanese realized they could use the jet stream to float bomb-laden balloons across the sea from Japan to the continental United States. But first they had to produce thousands of balloons.

While Japanese men assembled bombs, figuring out how to attach them to the balloons, and determined when they would need to drop, Japanese women were put to work making the balloons that would carry the bombs. By hand, they made a special kind of strong tissue paper called *washi* from the bark of mulberry trees. They formed the paper into different-size sheets, which were then glued together by hundreds of Japanese schoolgirls. Toshiko Inoue was one of those girls.

"It was work more difficult than you could ever imagine. We took sheets of *washi* and cut them on the board. Each piece was glued to another piece and left to dry. This process was repeated . . . until it was five layers thick."

Yaeko Yokomizo had vivid memories of the atmosphere: "We glued the *washi* together using a paste called *konnyaku* glue, prepared by adding water to a huge pot of glue and stirring for two hours. During the very hottest days, we worked where children [would normally have] parked their bikes and the playgrounds were used for drying." Food was in short supply because of the war, and groups of officers watched over hungry workers to make sure they were only doing their jobs and not eating any of the paste.

Hundreds of Japanese girls worked to cut sheets of *washi* paper and then glue pieces together to make thick layers for the balloon construction.

Japanese girls stand at the base of an inflated balloon. This photo could have been taken during the last stage of production, in which they would have painted on lacquer to waterproof the balloon. It also shows the scale of its size.

If it seems strange that schoolchildren were a labor force for weapons of war, Tetsuko Tanaka remembers that this was just how life was in Japan at that time: "My education stressed contributing to the war effort and being a patriot. . . . We were ordered not only to work but to lay down our lives for our country." Inoue agreed: "We worked each day to exhaustion, ate a tiny meal and went to bed. . . . There was no time left for thinking." Inoue's teacher told her, "Don't think too much about it. . . . Don't harbor any doubts. . . . Just do the work without complaining."

The Japanese military hoped that the balloon bombs would land in American forests and set them on fire. They assumed the fires would require immediate attention and take focus away from the war effort. American troops would be pulled away from what they were doing overseas to protect the home front, and panic would ensue. The Japanese also wanted to boost morale among their people. They wanted to show that they were doing everything possible to fight the enemy. To this end, the Japanese launched more than 9,000 balloon bombs. And then they waited.

And waited.

And waited.

Perhaps, the Japanese worried, it had all been for nothing. Their balloon-bomb project seemed to be a failure. Otherwise, they would certainly have begun to get word of explosions, fires, or at the very least, some of the balloons being spotted. In fact, the Japanese counted on what they perceived as the chatty nature of Americans to alert them that their bombs were indeed wreaking havoc. But the Americans weren't talking.

War Coming Right to Our Front Door

The silence was intentional. Just because Japan wasn't receiving any news reports or panic alerts about their balloon bombs didn't mean the U.S. military hadn't noticed. They just didn't want Japan to think their plan was working.

Reports of strange bomb sightings had been coming in since November 1944, when a U.S. Navy ship had pulled the remains of one on board. Other encounters had followed. A flash of light and the sound of an explosion outside her house startled a mother putting her child to bed one evening. A man and his son out chopping wood came across something that looked like a parachute. It turned out to be a Japanese balloon bomb.

Pieces of balloons were being recovered in many western states, including Wyoming, California, and Alaska, as well as parts of western Canada and northern Mexico. They were even found as far east as Michigan. In Oregon, soldiers were brought in to search for suspected remains of an unexploded balloon

This balloon was recovered near Davis, California, in March 1945. It helped the military reconstruct a complete unit to study. To create this photo, the photographer moved around the balloon with flashbulbs to illuminate it in eight places. The sandbags and incendiary bombs are hanging at right.

bomb. The scariest moment may well have been when a balloon got tangled in the electrical lines of an atomic energy plant (which happened to be making part of the atomic bomb that would later be dropped on Nagasaki) in Hanford, Washington, causing a brief power outage. It was quickly fixed, but it would have been disastrous if one of the bombs had detonated.

The press was asked to keep all these incidents quiet. *Newsweek* and *Time* magazines ran minor mentions, but the press generally did its part. The Japanese were fooled into thinking that their balloon bombs were not reaching America. That still didn't stop them from spreading rumors to the contrary. The Japanese broadcast to their nation, as well as parts of Europe and China, that their balloons had claimed hundreds of lives, caused many forest fires, and frightened the American people.

Of course, the people in Bly *had* been frightened. Once she was finally told what had happened, Diane Jordan, sister of one of the boys who was killed, said, "We knew we were at war, but the thought of war coming right to our front door never entered our minds." Shortly after those six deaths, officials did begin to lift the secrecy, at least in a small, controlled way. The military realized that the public needed to be quietly alerted to the danger, even though there was still a ban on major news stories.

This balloon was recovered near Alturas, California, on January 10, 1945. It was inflated for testing at Moffett Field at the naval base near San Francisco, California.

A Dodge to Avoid Using Us in Combat

The only truth in the announcements Japan made was the major concern the balloon bombs could set American forests on fire. The Naval Research Laboratory had been investigating the balloons, and as early as January 18, 1945, its officials stated: "It must be assumed that a considerable number are coming over. . . . When the dry season arrives considerable damage will result unless effective countermeasures are developed." It was clear that the authorities had to stay on top of this threat. They needed more men to deal with the situation.

Amid the threat of the balloon bombs, an unusually heavy lightning season, and the usual irresponsible campers, the Forest Service had its hands full.

Fully equipped to smokejump, a group of Triple Nickles is briefed by their jumpmaster at Pendleton, Oregon. Their gear includes helmet, wire face guard, two parachutes (main and reserve), first-aid kit, 150 feet of rope in case of a tree landing, personal kit, and boots. Shovels and other gear are dropped later.

It reached out to the military for help. The Air Force was called upon to shoot down the balloon bombs on sight, and the Triple Nickles were brought in to assist the firefighters.

Bradley Biggs reflected on the Triple Nickles' unusual transition to Operation Firefly: "[We had to] trade in our rifles . . . for a shovel . . . and a hoe. We weren't trained to do that." Nevertheless, the men wasted no time. "We've got a job to do, we've got orders, we've got a mission; that's it. We'll do it and we'll do it well."

That didn't mean they were happy about it.

"We felt it was a dodge to avoid using us in combat," Roger Walden said.

He may have been right.

In the meantime, they got to work.

"We were soldiers. We did what we had to do," Morris said.

We Stank of Smoke

Since smokejumping was a relatively new practice for the Forest Service, the Triple Nickles were on the cutting edge of learning this new method of fighting fires. It would require some additional training. First off, they had been taught to *avoid* trees, not jump down into them! And jumping into a forest lit up like a million candles was a far cry from dropping onto an open field.

The men were split into two groups: some stayed in Pendleton, Oregon, and others were sent to Chico, California. In May and June, they trained as firefighters and smokejumpers, and some—including Walden and Biggs—learned how to collect and dismantle the bombs. The Forest Service men were excellent teachers.

"They could walk up the hills like a cat," Biggs wrote. He was impressed. "They taught us how to climb, use an axe, and what vegetation to eat." Part of the 555th's training involved learning how to use a new kind of parachute designed by a smokejumper named Frank Derry. These so-called Derry chutes gave jumpers the ability to steer—a much-needed advantage when coming down into a sea of trees.

By July, the Triple Nickles were ready to be the U.S. Army's only smokejumpers.

To check how the wind was blowing, they watched which way the smoke shifted from the fire. When they jumped, they had to make sure not to hit any rocks or get tangled up in trees. They had traded in their paratrooper steel helmets for football helmets fitted with a simple square of wire mesh—the only thing keeping the branches from tearing up their faces.

Pendleton, Oregon, August 1945. There were only nine black parachute riggers in the Army, and they worked with the 555th. Packing a chute properly is serious business, and any rigger knew any trooper could ask him to jump with one of the chutes he packed.

A jump could put them down in the fire for days, so the supplies they needed—food, first-aid and fire-fighting equipment—had to be dropped, too. The amount of water it would have taken to fight a fire was too heavy to carry, so only enough water for drinking was dropped.

Before they could even start fighting a fire, they had to untangle their lines, shed their heavy jumpsuits, and pack up their gear. It was difficult for the men to breathe due to all the smoke. The fires were hot enough to singe their eyebrows.

Flames had to be put out, and hotspots covered. Hotspots are places where no fire is visible but the ground is so hot that it smokes. If these spots aren't covered, they can burst into flame at any second. Jordon "JJ" Corbett had joined the 555th in November 1944 and was among those who had traveled to Pendleton. "You could have a fire almost put out," he remembered, "and it would spark and then all of a sudden, zoom! A big fire would start back up."

Week after week, they put out fires. They searched for balloon bombs to dismantle.

Sometimes the fires were enormous. "The largest fire we had required a hundred men jumping at once," Walden remembered.

Sometimes it was so dark it was impossible to see the guy in front of you. It didn't matter how dark or hot or smoky it got; each man made sure no one got lost or swallowed up in the smoke. "We stank of smoke and fought to keep upwind of it," Biggs recalled.

At night, they took turns sleeping on the ground or being on watch. They had to look out for fire flare-ups or animals wandering into camp. "We had to fight rattlesnakes; we were fighting bears," Biggs said, his eyes opening wide at the thought. The bears had caught on fast that food was dropping from the sky

Triple Nickles member Clyde Thomas boards a Troop Carrier Command plane loaded down with all the equipment he needs for a fire-fighting mission.

After jumping near a fire with the 555th and setting up his stove—dropped by parachute—Sergeant Theodore Kaing puts on his chef clothes and begins cooking for the men.

and had started hightailing it to the Drop Zones. "We worked hard and ate like horses," Biggs said. It was no fun when the bears got to the food first.

Sometimes missions lasted four or five days and were many miles into the woods. "The area on fire could be twenty-five miles away from the road," Morris said. "These were really remote areas," Ted Lowry remembered. "We jumped in around the fire and contained it until the regular firefighters, who traveled on mules, could get up there."

At the end of a mission, they would pack up their gear and walk back to the base, miles out of the forest. Muscles aching, covered in grit and grime, all they wanted to do was rest their weary bones and sleep—after pouring cold drinks down their scorched throats.

But the club on the base wouldn't let them in. No coloreds allowed.

August 1945. The paratroopers dropped in on fires that would have taken days to reach otherwise. Here, Triple Nickles stomp out a fire and cover hotspots in an inaccessible part of the Umatilla National Forest.

A 555th trooper in Pendleton, Oregon, waits in full gear to board the C-47 in the background for a smokejumping mission.

CHAPTER EIGHT

THE ARMY HAD NO PLACE FOR US

After all they had done—and were doing—for their nation, the Triple Nickles were still not accepted as equal citizens. Nothing seemed to trump the color of their skin.

Biggs said that in Pendleton, a predominantly white town, "the reception was cold. We could not eat in any one of the restaurants." His voice held the chill of that memory. "[We] found it difficult," he said, "to buy a drink or a meal. Only two bars would serve [us] anything. We could not go into the hotel—they refused to give us a room. . . . Hotels in town would not serve us." The people there, he felt, "were living in the Northwest but with a southern attitude."

Morris agreed. His voice had a sad tone: "The townspeople in Pendleton were very negative in their attitude toward black soldiers."

It was not just the citizens who were less than happy to greet the men of the 555th. The colonel in command of Pendleton Air Base was, as Biggs portrayed in his book, "a man who would quickly make it clear that he disliked having an all-black unit at his station. He was careful that we did not mix with his officers, that our area was inspected with undue meticulousness, and that the

JJ Corbett (second from right) and fellow Triple Nickles in Pendleton, Oregon, summer 1945

atmosphere of his office was 'cool' to us." The men were upset that they "had to serve again under a prejudiced post commander. We had just left one at Mackall. . . . Such was our lot."

They Were a Fine Bunch to See

There were also positive interactions between blacks and whites. Clarence Beavers and JJ Corbett remember eating at the restaurants in town without incident. Beavers said he ate out all the time, enjoying the steak and chili that were popular out West. Corbett didn't have any trouble either, but the sign on the door that said "Indians and Dogs Not Allowed" upset him. The Triple Nickles had good experiences with the smokejumpers they trained and worked with side by side. "The smokejumpers we encountered with respect to the Forestry Service were also top flight guys. We had a wonderful relationship," Biggs said. They were not only welcoming; they were also extremely helpful in their roles as teachers to their new firefighting partners: "They told us what branches we could avoid . . . what foods we could eat, how to sleep, where to sleep, how to cut a tree down. . . . [It was a] wonderful relationship."

Although the general feeling in Pendleton seemed to be that the Triple Nickles should stay out of sight and stick to the base, some folks enjoyed seeing the men in town. Cathryn Davenport grew up in Pendleton and was impressed by their appearance.

"The most we saw of them was downtown . . . all dressed in full uniform . . . and it was not a planned event or anything—it was very spontaneous on their part. They would fall into formation and march to cadence down Main Street, and I tell you that was a showstopper. . . . They were a fine bunch to see." Biggs

Company A of the 555th assembled in Pendleton, Oregon

recollected that the men did venture into Pendleton once in a while to go to the movies. They even put on a few demonstration jumps for the locals. Corbett also remembered a group of them having a great time at a local rodeo event.

On one occasion, Biggs and some of his men were loaned to the Navy for a special mission to train a group of naval pilots who were about to be sent overseas. During this one-day operation, the lieutenant commander, paying no attention to segregation rules, took the men to lunch in the naval officers' club. "I could not help but notice," Biggs recollected, "that this sister service treated us better than our own."

Biggs realized that "perhaps we were jumping under conditions as close to combat as we might see."

The men served with distinction, taking the naval pilots through a simulation of jumping into battle during an enemy attack and fortifying ground troops with supplies. They jumped fully loaded with water, food, weapons, and ammunition on their backs. The Triple Nickles received high praise for this mission and became the first black paratroopers to serve with the U.S. Navy. During the mission, the hopeful but pragmatic Biggs was struck with the realization that "perhaps we were jumping under conditions as close to combat as we might see."

We Were Denied the Experience

Roger Walden was also skeptical about the 555th's chances of ever being given a combat mission. But the information they were given about the balloon bombs made him feel better about their assignment. "Upon arriving at our destination we learned that over a period of time . . . there had been a build-up of forest fires in the Northwest caused by incendiary bombs carried by balloons released by the Japanese . . . doing considerable damage in the great forests of . . . Canada and the United States."

Unbeknownst to Walden, however, this information was not completely accurate. For one thing, the bombs did not seem to be setting off many fires.

Opposite: Lieutenant Jesse Mayes. As jumpmaster, he was in command of his men on the ground and had to know when to make the drop. Here, he is about to jump out of a C-47 Troop Carrier Command plane.

When asked whether the Triple Nickles were given any specific knowledge that the fires they were fighting were actually set by the incendiary bombs, Morris said, "We could not confirm or deny that. Of the thirty-six fires we contained, I have no idea how many were started by the incendiary balloons. The rumor was there was very few."

In fact, according to meticulously charted information that later documented where and when every bomb was dropped, the Japanese balloon bombs were not responsible for any of the forest fires set that season.

And because no news reports or panic alerts about the effectiveness of their balloon bombs ever got back to the Japanese, they had assumed that their efforts had failed. The Japanese had canceled the balloon-bomb project in mid-April, before the 555th even arrived. This may be why two of the most respected scholarly books on Japanese balloon bombs do not give the Triple Nickles much attention. *Japanese Paper Balloon Bombs* refers only to two hundred paratroopers who were part of a larger effort; *Silent Siege* does not discuss them at all. And *A Pictorial History of Smokejumping*, endorsed by the U.S. Forest Service, briefly mentions the 555th but reports that "the battalion was never used for balloon fires."

Even though the fires the 555th fought were not caused by balloon bombs, their firefighting service was greatly needed. Both the threat of the bombs and the 555th's additional duties were extremely dangerous and real. Walden can confirm that firsthand: "We did find a few of the magnesium bombs that had failed to ignite, or fragments which we carried back to our base for further study and further training." JJ Corbett also had a close encounter with a bomb. "We found a bomb that had not detonated—it was still hanging in the brush on its balloon. So we were trained in dealing [with] and disposing of the bombs."

The Triple Nickles also played an integral part in pioneering the field of smokejumping as they dropped into the blazes and put them out. They tested equipment and techniques that are now standard smokejumping practices. There were injuries, including some broken bones, but the Triple Nickles suffered only one casualty. Malvin L. Brown was the only member of the 555th to die in the line of duty during World War II. In all, between July and October 1945, the 555th made 1,200 jumps and helped control 36 fires.

But questions remain as to why the 555th was the only group of paratroopers chosen to do this important work. What was really going on behind the scenes? Did the existence of the bombs create a perfect opportunity for the military to appease the Triple Nickles with an important noncombat assignment? Why was there such a rapid and secret need for the 555th to report to Oregon for Operation Firefly? Was it a diversion to keep these black troops from being sent overseas? Some of the 555th certainly felt that way.

About being shipped out west, Morris said, "This was like a godsend for the Army because they didn't know what to do with us. . . . The Army had no place for us. None of the commanding generals wanted the extra problem of integrating colored soldiers with the white soldiers, so they refused."

This is the bomb-carrying part of the balloon apparatus. Bags of sand were hung from an aluminum wheel. At different altitudes, sandbags would be dropped to make the balloon rise higher. The Japanese calculated the speed and distance of the balloon so that once all the sandbags were dropped, the balloon should have been located over the American West, and the bombs were released. The black cylindrical objects hanging near the sandbags are the bombs.

The Army Had No Place for Us **91**

August 1945. Triple Nickles Captain Richard Williams and Lieutenant Clifford Allen look through the open door to pick the spot where they will drop Lieutenant Harry Sutton (bareheaded and smiling at left) and his team. Sutton went on to earn a Silver Star for gallantry in action in the Korean War, in which he lost his life.

He explained further in a phone interview: "General MacArthur did not want any colored paratroops in the Pacific; he did not want the additional job of integrating the services. It had never been done, and he had other important things to do, he thought, with winning the Pacific theater combat. He didn't want us, and that was a blow to us, as well as the one that we got when we thought we were going overseas. None of the commanders wanted any colored troops. It had not been done. They didn't know what would happen when they brought black and white soldiers together. We were denied the experience."

Perhaps sending the 555th to smokejump and fight fires was the best use of their time and skills as the war in Europe was coming to a close. But one could argue that instead of being sent to Europe, the 555th could have been deployed to the Pacific. On the other hand, the sequence of events that led to America's dropping the atomic bomb on Japan—which quickly ended the war—was already in place by July 1945, so it is possible the military commanders already knew they would likely not need more troops.

It may be impossible to ever know definitive answers to some of these questions. But the importance and value of what the Triple Nickles achieved is clear, and their accomplishments carved out a new path that others would follow.

This Is My Country, My Children's Country, and Their Children's

One sunny August morning, about to smokejump into another forest fire, Walter Morris stood in the open door of the plane and thought about the discrimination he and his men faced. "Why, I asked, was I standing here on my way to a dangerous mission that could possibly get me and my men killed? Why should I die for a country that thought so little of me and my people?"

Morris thought about all that he and the Triple Nickles had accomplished since he had first marched his men onto that calisthenics field in Fort Benning two years earlier. He thought about how their spirits had lifted as they had begun to realize they were just as skilled and able as the white paratrooper students. He flashed back to being called to General Gaither's office and getting the surprising news that a black paratrooper company was going to be formed. His mind raced back over earning his silver wings, officer school, combat training, smokejumping training, and firefighting.

They had done all that, even when people thought they shouldn't. Even when people made bets that they wouldn't. Morris looked down at the raging fire.

> **Why would a black man risk his life to help his country?**

"I was struck with a sudden understanding of my reason for being there. Why would a black man risk his life to help his country? The answer was simple. This is my country; this is my duty regardless of the social climate; regardless of the faults. This is my country, my children's country, and their children's. It is up to me and many, many people of all races and cultures to fight the haters and racists to make this a better place to live."

The 555th proudly participated in parades celebrating the Armed Services and America's victory in WWII. In this photograph the 555th marches down Michigan Avenue in Chicago for the Army Day Parade on April 6, 1946.

CHAPTER NINE

WE WILL HAVE A COLORLESS SOCIETY ONE DAY

January 12, 1946, began as a gray, rainy morning. More than 12,000 paratroopers of the 82nd Airborne were about to march down New York City's Fifth Avenue for a victory parade celebrating the end of World War II. As the parade got under way, sunshine burst through the clouds. A brass band blared John Philip Sousa's rousing "Stars and Stripes Forever," and more than two million people started to cheer from the sidelines and the balconies of buildings along the parade route. Nearly 350 Triple Nickles marched right alongside the 82nd Airborne. They all—members of the 555th included—wore colorful honors across their chests, decorations from 82nd Airborne victories during the war.

Three of the 555th who marched that day later shared vivid memories. Melvin Lester said, "Black people in the crowd went crazy and were coming out to greet us." They were mentioned in the paper the next day, and Lester said, "I kept that . . . until it turned brown and crumbled up!" Carstell Stewart was pensive. "It was a heck of a feeling that we were there. It was like goose pimples, and that sort of situation." Jesse Mayes smiled and waved his hands in the air as he thought back. "Oh, you should have been there. When we came down

Captain James Porter leads the 555th down Fifth Avenue in New York City as part of the victory parade on January 12, 1946. They marched with the 82nd Airborne.

that street . . . man, they were yelling . . . and we were strutting down there like peacocks." He laughed long and hard. "I tell you, that was a great feeling."

The man responsible for this feeling was General James Gavin. As Walter Morris said, it was up to many people to challenge racism and change the world. Gavin would loom large as one of those people.

A Two-Colored Army

Five months earlier, on August 14, 1945, the Japanese had surrendered. World War II was over. The Triple Nickles had continued to fight fires for the Forest Service until October, when Operation Firefly came to an end. They were then reassigned to the 13th Airborne Division and sent to Fort Bragg, North Carolina.

Once again, the Triple Nickles were given inferior housing, in an area Gavin later described as "a mud pond surrounded by sand." Gavin wrote that the Triple Nickles "were billeted in old tar-paper-covered shacks for barracks. Their swimming pool was not much more than a mud puddle and their bathhouse was a scandal." Once again, the Triple Nickles were kept out of the recreation center and the Officers' Club for white soldiers, so once again, they started their own. Gavin saw that the Triple Nickles "did well with what it had been given," but it caused him a great deal of concern.

It upset Gavin—whom Biggs described as "color-blind"—that, in his own words, "our Army had been a two-colored Army for a long time, just as was our society." At thirty-eight, Gavin had served with the all-black 25th Infantry and had experienced firsthand how black soldiers were just as "well trained, well armed, and well led" as white soldiers. Gavin decided to take action and find a way to integrate the Triple Nickles into the 82nd Airborne. Knowing that what he was going to ask for had never been done before, and that he would likely be rejected if he simply wrote a letter of request, Gavin went right to the top. He traveled to Washington, D.C., and had a meeting with Lieutenant General John Hull in the War Department.

Major General James M. Gavin

After Gavin had stated his case, Hull addressed him.

"General," Hull asked, "do you intend to give all those . . . medals that the 82nd won in Europe to the 555th?"

Gavin said yes, and added that, if the 555th were integrated into the 82nd, they would benefit from the "newest equipment and weapons" he knew the 82nd was getting and so would have the opportunity to earn those honors for themselves. "I'll see to that," Gavin told Hull.

And so the Triple Nickles marched in the victory parade wearing those medals. Gavin began working with the 555th at Fort Bragg in early 1946.

On December 9, 1947, the 555th was officially integrated into the 82nd Airborne as the 3rd Battalion of the 505th Parachute Infantry Brigade, under Gavin's leadership.

It was an emotional day. Triple Nickles member William Weathersbee remembers it well: "I walked in the barracks, and it was as if someone had died." It was also fresh for Charles Stevens, who joined the 555th in 1946: "Everybody

Major General Gavin with 2nd Lieutenant Roger S. Walden as they view the Drop Zone during a training jump near Fort Bragg, North Carolina, in 1946. This was Gavin's first jump with the 555th.

was crying. . . . I think we were crying for two different reasons. We were glad that segregation was leaving the Army, and we were sad we were losing our Triple Nickles colors." Stevens said of the 555th: "I finally felt like I belonged to something."

They were now the first black unit to be integrated into an airborne division, as well as into a white division. But Gavin couldn't have done it without the record that the Triple Nickles brought with them. Military historian Bernard Nalty said, "There's no question that Gavin played a critical role, but you've got to remember you had good people in the 555th. And what they did, they did by themselves, for themselves. . . . No one is going to adopt an outfit that is weak, and Gavin may have had the greatest moral instincts in the world but if this was not a good fighting outfit he would have had nothing to do with it." Still, Biggs wrote that the Triple Nickles' appearance in the victory parade was "a symbol of Gavin's determination to proceed with racial integration in the service."

"But he did more than that," Biggs insisted. Once Gavin integrated the Triple Nickles into the 82nd Division, he also placed several of the 555th men in leadership roles in different companies. "Now," Biggs said, his admiration for Gavin coming through loud and clear, "when you had that happening, you had a sprinkling, *then*, of integration under Jim Gavin [in] now all of his key staff division positions." Biggs also said Gavin "moved quickly to provide equal treatment for his black officers and men." Integration under Gavin was not going to be halfhearted. With pride brimming in his voice, Morris emphatically said, "White soldiers and black soldiers moved into the same barracks. . . . That was historic. . . . And there was not one incident of racism—not one."

White soldiers and black soldiers moved into the same barracks. . . . That was historic.

Taken at Fort Bragg in 1946 or 1947, two of the original 555th test platoon
are shown here—Hubert Bridges and Jack Tillis (second and third from left).

I Had No Idea It Was As Terrible As That

On April 12, 1945, Franklin Delano Roosevelt died and Vice President Harry S. Truman—who had held that position for only eighty-two days—was sworn in as president. After the war, Truman had to tackle many domestic problems, one of which was that the equal rights of African Americans needed to be upheld. His record as a senator showed that he had supported antilynching bills and antidiscrimination investigations and had spoken out in favor of equal opportunities for African Americans. In his memoirs, Truman reflected, "I was raised amidst some violently prejudiced Southerners myself," yet he believed that "the vast majority of good southerners understand that the blind prejudices of past generations cannot continue in a free republic."

Truman, who came from Missouri, also knew that anything he did for the African-American population could help his chances of getting their vote in the next election. Perhaps most important, Truman began to realize that equality could never be achieved while segregation remained a reality. He also recognized that it was time for the American people to "practice what they preached, since the world was watching."

What the world saw often wasn't pretty. Unlike the favorable experience the Triple Nickles had in the victory parade, black soldiers returning home from combat—including some of the 555th—were often not given a hero's welcome. JJ Corbett had a stopover at a train station on his way home. Strong and tall, in his spotless paratrooper uniform, he strode toward a café but was stopped from entering through the front door. He and his buddy got back on the train. A soldier from the 92nd Infantry, James Tillman, looked back on his own unit's homecoming: "We landed in Norfolk, Virginia. We were all Buffalo Soldiers, and they didn't want us to go through the town. They said it would cause too much traffic, but I knew it was because we were black, and that hurt. We waited there on the docks for two hours with no facilities, and finally our officers said we could walk the five miles to the camp. . . . We were the first troops home, but no one clapped or cheered. The whole town was white and

We were the first troops home, but no one clapped or cheered.

had we been white, they would have mobbed us, they would have been so happy."

Far worse, some particularly violent attacks on black World War II veterans in 1946 made it clear that it was time to take action. Truman addressed the NAACP directly, saying, "I had no idea it was as terrible as that. We've got to do something." On December 6 of that year, Truman created the President's Committee on Civil Rights. He said, "When we fail to live together in peace, the failure touches not us, as Americans alone, but the cause of democracy itself in the whole world."

The wheels did not turn as quickly as promised, but the committee worked hard and by January 1948, Truman decided it was time to take it upon himself to end segregation in the military by executive order. On July 26, 1948, he signed Executive Order 9981. Of course, the Triple Nickles had already pioneered that front, having been integrated into the 82nd Airborne a full seven months earlier.

"It is hereby declared," the order read, "to be the policy of the president that there shall be equality of treatment and opportunity for all persons in the armed services without regard to race, color, religion or national origin. This policy shall be put into effect as rapidly as possible and having due regard to the time required to effectuate any necessary changes without impairing efficiency or morale."

Truman's intention to ensure equality between blacks and whites was real, but his personal beliefs about integration were not as clear. He wrote to a southern friend who questioned his stance on civil rights, "I am not asking for social equality because no such thing exists, but I am asking for equality of opportunity for all human beings, and as long as I stay here, I am going to continue that fight."

"We served together but had to be scattered and drift home in little units because of segregation," Ashley Bryan remembers. He drew this pen-and-ink sketch of a good friend in his company, completely dismayed by the news they had just received.

This fuzziness would have its consequences. Neither the word *integration* nor the word *segregation* was included in his executive order. This left the document open to interpretation—and, therefore, resistance. It took a while longer, but by January 16, 1950, when the Army's integration plan was finally approved, each branch of the armed services had begun to integrate. Within three years, the Army announced that 95 percent of African-American soldiers were serving in integrated units.

> *It proves what we were—American soldiers.*

Irving Dickerson didn't join the all-black paratroop unit (then designated the 505th) until 1949, but he had served during World War II in another all-black unit that was sent to Italy and used for security work, before finally being given the chance to fight on the front lines. Dickerson had this to say about integration: "It proves what we were—American soldiers. Not black soldiers but American soldiers."

It Started to Make Americans Ashamed of Their Attitudes

World War II was truly a turning point in American race relations. Historian Charles E. Silberman said this was the time in which "the seeds of the protest movements of the 1950s and 1960s were sown." White Americans found it difficult to ignore the fact that they had been fighting Hitler while perpetrating atrocities and inequalities on their own black citizens—especially when those black citizens had done their part to unite in the fight against the same foe. "[African Americans] made a significant contribution to the war effort at home and abroad," historian Stephen Ambrose has written. "It started to make Americans ashamed of their attitudes."

Add this shame to the fact that black Americans were no longer willing to stomach discrimination without protest. They were determined to fight for better status in American society. One soldier said that when he came home after the war, "I carried myself in a different way after I came back, and people could tell." Integration of the military, Biggs said, also made it possible for "the civilian population . . . to see that their white sons would be led by a black soldier. . . . So these white soldiers would go home and say, 'Mom, Dad, my squad leader is a black soldier. He's my friend; I respect and admire him.' That is our success. That's where the civil-rights attitude comes from, and that's where we as black servicemen helped remove a cancer that was part of American society . . . born in segregation and discrimination."

Another Triple Nickles member, Joe Murchison, joined the 555th not long before it became part of the 82nd. He witnessed the effect integration had, too: "The individual soldiers . . . started interacting with each other and going home on pass together and meeting each other's families, and that led to acceptance." This was the whole key to a change in race relations. Once black and white people began having real experiences together, instead of just imagining them, it took some of the fear out of the situation.

One major event that had a positive impact on life for returning veterans was the passing of the GI Bill of Rights, which helped soldiers pay for education as well as housing. These rights belonged to every veteran regardless of race and effectively increased the educational opportunities available to blacks. Triple Nickles member Samuel Robinson studied business at Roosevelt College on the GI Bill and went to law school after that. Soldier Alex Pitcher said, "Before World War II, there wasn't too much interest in any of us. . . . Most

Black Americans were no longer willing to stomach discrimination without protest.

of us didn't have the chance to become doctors or lawyers. . . . So our eyes were opened all across this country. . . . We became aware of the racial problem, and we became aware of what to do about it."

Ashley Bryan, now an award-winning author and illustrator of children's books, returned from his service as a stevedore in the Army during World War II to finish the college degree in art he had started at Cooper Union before being drafted. "Like most veterans, I was so spun around," he said. "I wanted to understand why we select war, even though we know the tragedies and destruction that

Left: An image from Spike Lee's *Miracle at St. Anna,* a movie in which Lee highlighted the heroics of black soldiers in World War II

Right: Actor George C. Scott, playing General Patton in the movie about Patton's life. African-American actor James Edwards played Patton's orderly, George Meeks. Edwards had gained fame twenty years earlier for landing a mainstream role in *Home of the Brave* and was known for speaking out against Hollywood stereotypes.

come with it." The GI Bill allowed Bryan to go on to study philosophy at Columbia University and art in Germany and France on a Fulbright Scholarship.

The NAACP quickly became involved anytime a college tried to deny a black veteran his or her rights under the GI Bill. Alex Pitcher was one veteran the NAACP went to bat for. He said, "We realized that black people never could really accomplish their dreams unless they had education." After he became a lawyer, Pitcher fought antidiscrimination battles for others.

Long after the war, some old military injustices were put right. Although not a single African-American soldier from World War II had ever been given a Medal of Honor—the highest military decoration for heroism—President Bill Clinton awarded seven of these medals to World War II veterans in 1997 (only one recipient was still living). And remember the 761st all-black battalion, which fought valiantly in the Battle of the Bulge but was denied its Distinguished Unit Citation? In 1978, President Jimmy Carter finally signed that citation for them, and they were given their due. Yet eight years earlier, the movie *Patton* was released, with no mention of the 761st at all, even though Patton, who was against integration, had agreed to take them, saying, "I would never have asked for you if you weren't good. . . . I don't care what color you are, so long as you go up there and kill those Kraut [German] sonsabitches. . . . Your race is looking forward to your success. Don't let them down." Although this episode of history is well documented, only one black man—Patton's orderly—is portrayed in an entire movie dedicated to this general's life.

The 1998 film *Saving Private Ryan,* as well as the 2001 miniseries *Band of Brothers,* also failed to give credit to black soldiers. Famous black director Spike Lee did something about that in 2008, with his movie *Miracle at St. Anna,* which focuses on four soldiers from the 92nd Infantry Division. Although it is a fictional story, Lee's motivation was to add black soldiers to their rightful place in history. "In World War II movies," Lee said, "rarely do you see black men in the picture at all, never mind being heroic." In a classic scene, one of the film's main characters speaks directly to why the role of the black soldier is so important to acknowledge: "They said we couldn't fight. Had us float balloons, work as quartermasters, cook and clean, but the 92nd proved we can fight. This is our country, too. We helped build it from the ground up."

The Color of a Man Had Nothing to Do with His Ability

As for the legacy of the Triple Nickles, it lives on strong today. The three surviving members of the original test platoon—Walter Morris, Roger Walden, and Clarence Beavers—are still educating people about their experiences. "We didn't win any wars, but we did contribute," Morris has said. "What we proved was that the color of a man had nothing to do with his ability."

In 2004, sixty years after Morris earned his wings, his grandson, Michael Fowles, became a paratrooper, too. Morris had the honor of bestowing his own silver wings on his grandson. He was also the guest speaker at the ceremony, which took place at Fort Benning.

"When he pinned on my wings," Fowles remarked, "he said he was proud of me and this was one of the best days of his life. Then he said he'd kill me

Walter Morris stands with his grandson, Michael Fowles, after Fowles earned his paratrooper wings.

if I lost his wings. I said I would protect them with my life." Morris was so overcome with emotion that he broke military protocol and hugged his grandson right then and there.

Morris said his grandson was momentarily embarrassed, but he got over it quickly. "I always looked up to him," Fowles said, "not only for what he did in the military, but for what he did as a man for his family and the community. He sacrifices a lot of time for other people."

Morris ended his term of service in January 1946, after the 555th had returned to Fort Bragg. Married, and with a young daughter, he decided to retire from the military. He and his family moved first to Seattle, where his father taught him the trade of bricklaying, and later to New York City, where his mother was. There he became one of the first African Americans in the bricklayers' union and managed construction projects, often for the city of New York. He now lives in Florida, where he was an early organizer of the African American Cultural Society in Palm Coast.

Clarence Beavers worked for the Veterans Administration until 1959 and then went to Germany for a job with the Department of Defense. He retired in 1979 and now lives in New York State. Roger Walden remained in the Army and was promoted to major in 1955 and to lieutenant colonel in 1962. He retired from the military four years later and now lives in Michigan. Many of the other 555th members who stayed in the Army went on to earn promotions and to fight valiantly in the Korean War, and later in the Vietnam War. Several, including Roger Walden, received the Silver Star for their service.

Bradley Biggs enjoyed a long and distinguished career in the Army. After the war ended, Biggs took part in operations for the 82nd Airborne. He then went on to serve in Korea. Biggs retired in 1961 and spent much of his later career working in different areas of education, including serving as dean of faculty at Middlesex Community College. Biggs also focused on furthering his own education, earning two master's degrees from Wesleyan University.

They Took the Door off the Hinges

Decades after General James Gavin took the 555th under his wing, in 2010, Gavin's grandson had a chance to reflect on his actions. Staff Sergeant Joseph Gavin said, "I'm proud my grandfather recognized the talents of these soldiers and helped integrate them into the 82nd Airborne. They paved the way for all soldiers who followed them."

Sam Day, a paratrooper in the 11th Airborne who fought in the Korean War, agreed: "They opened the door for young black paratroopers." A veteran of the Vietnam War, Robert Sample, echoed this sentiment: "I'm not concerned about whether they went to combat. . . . If I didn't know about the Triple Nickles, I would never have thought about going to jump school." William Smith also served in Vietnam, in the Army's Airborne Division, and credits his success to these pioneers: "Just as the Tuskegee Airmen opened the way for black pilots," he said, "the Triple Nickles opened the way for blacks to become paratroopers."

The trail the 555th pioneered was not just about paratroopers or smokejumpers. It was about the way people considered race. "When you look out at the Army of today," Morris said, "it's such a pleasure because it's such a difference. You see white, black, red, yellow all doing their job." Triple

Clarence Beavers, April 2008

Nickle Joe Murchison says that his experience in the 82nd Airborne changed how he thought about race. "I don't answer to African-American. I'm All-American." After retiring from the Army in 1960, Murchison became a businessman.

Murchison was one of the founders of the 555th Parachute Infantry Association in 1979 and invited General Gavin to give the first keynote speech. The association honors the Triple Nickles by maintaining the battalion's history and enabling members to keep in touch with one another. The association even has a jump team. Murchison's dignity and delight shines through whenever he talks about the Triple Nickles. "When the 555th was folded into the 505th and changed the name, it was an end of an era for the men who were involved," he said. He serves as the association's president, and membership is open to any paratrooper, regardless of race. There are chapters all over the country. Sam Day ran a chapter in Philadelphia and was proud of its diversity. "Anybody can join the Triple Nickles now as long as they're Airborne," he said. "White, black, green—anybody."

In July 2000, the fifty-fifth anniversary of Operation Firefly was celebrated. By 2009, museums at Fort Benning and Fort Bragg included Triple Nickles exhibits. In February 2003, the Triple Nickles were honored with a granite monument placed at the entrance of the Airborne & Special Operations Museum in Fayetteville, North Carolina. Engraved with the names of the first twenty-three members, the monument proudly calls attention to the historical significance of this outstanding unit. The curator, Mary Dennings, said, "We think it's important that soldiers know their history. They need to know where they came from so they can be inspired to be the best soldiers they can be." Carstell Stewart would have agreed. With a set jaw and a look of determination, he talked about

making sure this history is not forgotten. He said, "The man with no history, the race with no history, has no future."

On March 26, 2010, the U.S. Forest Service honored the 555th for its heroic service to the agency. The day before, the Army had paid tribute to the 555th in a ceremony at the Pentagon. Morris, Beavers, and Walden attended both events. Everywhere these remaining heroes go, the theme of "opening the door" is repeated. Michele Jones, a paratrooper and retired command sergeant major, said, "These three gentlemen . . . kicked open the door; they took the door off the hinges. . . . [They] profoundly changed the course of history."

Present-day smokejumpers from Idaho and Montana traveled to Washington, D.C., to attend the ceremony there. As distinguished as ever at eighty-nine years old, Morris focused his light-brown eyes and easy smile on the jumpers as he reminisced. Smokejumper Jesse Burns said, "It was so awesome. They are some of the pioneers, and it was great to listen to their stories."

General David Petraeus and Walter Morris pose with a statue modeled after Morris following the unveiling on September 7, 2006, at Fort Leavenworth, Kansas. It honors all the members of the first and only all-black World War II parachute battalion.

There is a 555th monument at Fort Benning, as part of the Airborne Walk, and another marking the exact spot where the 555th graduated. At the time of this writing, funds are being raised for a larger monument to be built for the new National Infantry Museum.

At his paratrooper graduation, Walter Morris's grandson may have said it best for all who follow in the 555th's footsteps: "There's a great responsibility on my shoulders. I have to represent [my grandfather] well . . . with dignity and respect." It is respect for all people, in fact, that propels change. As with any story about people who challenge stereotypes and push boundaries, growth didn't stop with the Triple Nickles. More milestones went on to be achieved—in the face of more setbacks.

General George W. Casey Jr. (left) talks with Roger Walden at the March 25, 2010, event at the Pentagon. During his military career, Walden fought in the Korean War and rose to the rank of lieutenant colonel.

Today, African Americans make up 17 percent of the armed forces. To date, there have been only ten black four-star generals. One of those is Colin Powell—an honorary Triple Nickle—who went on to make history as the first African-American chairman of the Joint Chiefs of Staff and the first black U.S. secretary of state. History was made again when Barack Obama became president in 2008. About that landmark moment, Triple Nickle Ted Lowry said, "To tell you the truth, I never thought I'd live to see the day that a black man became president. This will be something that we'll never forget."

Improvements still need to be made. Prejudice is a flaw of human nature, but awareness and education are powerful weapons against it. The Army now has an equal opportunity program to protect against discrimination of all kinds. Hubert Bridges Jr. took after his father—one of the original test platoon members. He became a paratrooper and military man as well and went on to serve as the director of military equal opportunity in Washington, D.C.

There has been a major shift in thinking since the days of World War II, when the top brass was not necessarily sympathetic to the issue of equality. As African-American General Lloyd J. Austin, who became Vice Chief of Staff of the U.S. Army in 2012, said, "We treasure diversity because it brings in a lot of different viewpoints and blends in a lot of cultures. It makes us better."

Progress is not perfect. It is not achieved quickly. There will be setbacks, but the hope is that there will always also be forward movement. The story of the Triple Nickles is a shining example of that hope.

Barack Obama honors Lincoln's commitment to racial equality by giving a speech during his inaugural celebration in the shadow of the Lincoln Memorial.

INTEGRATION IN ACTION

Beginning with the Korean War, the U.S. military has been integrated. There is still progress to be made, but the process is headed in the right direction. The military now includes Americans of all races, as well as accepting women as equal participants in the armed forces.

Above: This 2012 graduating class of paratroopers from The Parachute School in Fort Benning, Georgia, shows a typical class, which now includes women as well as people of color.

Opposite above: November 20, 1950. An integrated unit of the 2nd Infantry Division during the Korean War.

Opposite below: Black and white soldiers fought together in the Vietnam War. These men are part of the 173rd Airborne Brigade. June 1966.

In the words of Walter Morris, "We succeeded where we were not expected
to succeed. And we overcame the pitfalls that were put there. We overcame. And
it's a warm feeling to know that, that color has nothing to do with it. It's what's in
one's heart. One's spirit. And that . . . should be a lesson to all of us. We should
have, and we will have, a colorless society one day. And that will be the crowning
jewel in this great country's history."

A group of Triple Nickles assembles by a Troop Carrier Command plane in the summer of 1945. Between July and October 1945, they bravely made 1,200 smokejumps and helped control 36 fires.

THE STORY BEHIND THE STORY

This has perhaps been my hardest book to write to date. Tiny bits and pieces of this story have been scattered in obscure places for decades. There have been articles written about the Triple Nickles, as well as one slim book by Bradley Biggs, which is primarily an autobiographical perspective, but putting all the events and the complete story together in historical context has never been done. Telling this whole story for the first time from beginning to end was a huge challenge as well as a thrill. My hope is that by sharing it, the Triple Nickles will become a well-known part of history. After all, at its peak, there were about 1,400 men who were part of the groundbreaking 555th.

THE RESEARCH

I would like to share a little about how I researched and wrote this book. First, there was much I had to leave out. The topics of military history, black military history, and race are enormous ones, and they have been written about in great detail in scores of books, many of which I read. But it is impossible to examine all of that history here. My focus remained on the Triple Nickles, so I chose parts of the larger history that were needed to give readers the context to better understand the importance of this story. I used many different sources to put the pieces of the puzzle together: books and articles, letters, presidential documents, audio interviews, documentary short videos and full-length movies, print interviews, direct conversations, and photographs.

There were times when I got sidetracked for days by the overwhelming amount of information about discrimination in the military and in our society. The section on Japanese balloon bombs alone was a fascinating month-long diversion. And then there were the letters from soldiers detailing violence and pleas for investigations, as well as from those who were convinced that if they contributed to a victory overseas, they would return to a country that would embrace them for what they were—Americans who had risked their lives for the ideals our nation is based on. But more often than not, that didn't happen.

Sometimes I had to make decisions about what to do with stories told over the years by men remembering things that happened to them forty, fifty, sixty, or seventy years in the past. For example, Ted Lowry's several accounts of the German POWs taunting him on a bus contained some inconsistencies, but they had to do with whether the event took place on a public bus or a military bus. The emotional truth of the story was strong and intact no matter when he told it.

Another interesting thing occurred when I was trying to figure out who the three test platoon men were who did not graduate (twenty began training, seventeen earned their wings). It is generally accepted that one of them, Emerald Jones, was the man who did not jump from the thirty-four-foot tower and became the company's mess cook. But who were the other two? Unofficial lists included a few names in addition to the ones I knew, but there were errors in some of those lists. I needed to be sure. After repeated conversations with surviving members and examination of the original payroll list for the 555th from June 1944, I was able to confirm that the last two men were James S. Williams and Cleo Washington. That alone was an exciting detail to nail down! But I still didn't know what caused each of them to leave the program—although I did know that one of them sustained a groin injury.

Then came a conversation with Clarence Beavers, who had a vivid memory of one of the two men being unwilling to leave the "sweat shed" and board the plane for one of the qualifying jumps. This was news to me! Clarence didn't remember the man's name, but he did say that Walter Morris was there as well, and the two of them had asked the man if he wanted any help. So I called Walter. Walter did not remember the man. OK, I had to accept that I had done all I could and my time for making changes was up. But a few hours later, the phone rang. It was Walter's daughter, and I could hear Walter talking in the background, saying the words "groin injury" and "James S. Williams." Eureka! I had never once spoken the names Cleo Washington or James S. Williams to him as I didn't want to plant those seeds, but his memory had triumphed and Walter was certain that Williams had suffered a groin injury. That left Cleo Washington as the man in the sweat shed! Mystery solved.

Now I had another decision to make. Amend the text, or tell this story here.

I chose the latter because, although the pieces had finally fallen in place, and I was as sure as I could be about them, taking into account margin of error is important. What if I was wrong? These are real people, with surviving family members, not just names in a book. Part of being a responsible narrator means not forgetting that. Better to tell the story here, in the context of sharing with readers how exciting researching and writing nonfiction can be, than to make that type of an error.

As you can surmise, I was able to speak with a few of the 555th many times, especially Walter Morris, Clarence Beavers, and Joe Murchison, and it was my great honor to get to know them. Walter actually read my initial version of this story for the first time in 2003, when it was still in picture-book form. Eventually, I came around to the realization—with the help of savvy editors Hilary Van Dusen and Marc Aronson, as well as Sarah Aronson, who insisted I stop being stubborn about keeping it a picture book—that the story needed to be told in long-form nonfiction, so I dug back into the research and started again. (This is the same process I went through with my book *Almost Astronauts,* so perhaps this is simply what I must do to find where I am going.) I am so grateful that Walter Morris was able and willing to read this version for me again in 2012, at the ripe young age of ninety-one.

THE IMAGES

My research extended beyond the text to include finding all the photographs—of which there are 103—and there were times I thought I might have to get a degree in detective work to complete it. At one point a smokejumper out in Missoula, Montana, was ready to crack a safe for me to get to some old photos his predecessor was sure were in there (thanks, Wayne Williams and Dan Cottrell!). The image selection process is as crucial to the authorial process as writing is. I spent a few years—off and on—looking for any archive or minor museum that might have an image or two related to the 555th, as well as locating surviving family members in hopes that their photo albums might yield just one image of a Triple Nickle.

Once I had exhausted my photo possibilities, the process of choosing each image to best help me tell the multiple layers of this story took several months. Finding some of these photographs was like uncovering hidden jewels or buried treasure—images that had been in shoe boxes, obscure archives, family scrapbooks. Those images that were loaned to me from some of the men's families are the images you see treated with a white border. And one of these pictures (on page 8) led to an exciting and unexpected development! Walter loaned me that photo, which was taken in front of the house where he and his young family had lived at Fort Benning. Historian Ed Howard had been trying to locate Walter's house for some time, but Walter couldn't remember the address. When I sent Ed the layouts to review for me, Ed quickly got in touch to ask if there was any more to the picture. I sent him the whole image and he was ecstatic. An hour later, he had enlarged the front stoop, analyzed specific cracks and chips in it, compared it to a front stoop on the street in question, and—bingo—Walter's house was found! Ed plans to have a historic marker put there. The power of research!

And then there is the artwork created by Ashley Bryan while he was a soldier in World War II. In addition to Walter Morris, Ashley also read my picture-book version way back in 2003, and then graciously read it again in 2012, in its present long-form. After the second reading, Ashley and I talked, and then he sent me some of the artwork he had made during the war. Scan after scan began arriving in my inbox. I was overwhelmed by his generosity and excited by what his images could add to this story. As with all the images in this book, I have been entrusted with them and have tried to hold them in their greatest light.

As I finished writing this story on a sunny Memorial Day morning, I was struck by how much more that national holiday now means to me. That was the morning I knew to whom this book would be dedicated. I feel privileged to have been able to take the time to put this story together and share it, in hopes that the Triple Nickles will become a more permanent and vivid part of the fabric that is our American history.

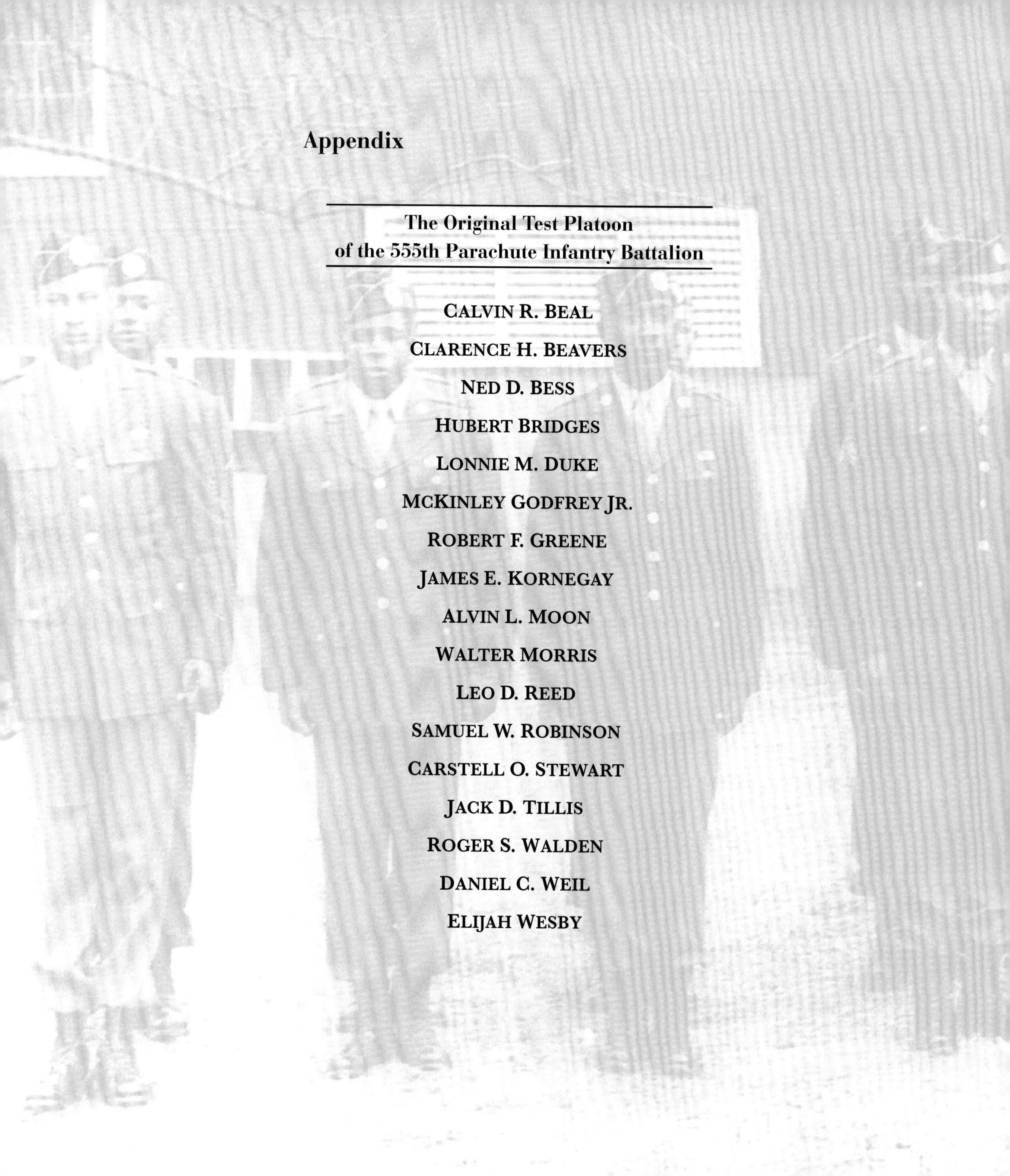

Appendix

The Original Test Platoon
of the 555th Parachute Infantry Battalion

CALVIN R. BEAL

CLARENCE H. BEAVERS

NED D. BESS

HUBERT BRIDGES

LONNIE M. DUKE

MCKINLEY GODFREY JR.

ROBERT F. GREENE

JAMES E. KORNEGAY

ALVIN L. MOON

WALTER MORRIS

LEO D. REED

SAMUEL W. ROBINSON

CARSTELL O. STEWART

JACK D. TILLIS

ROGER S. WALDEN

DANIEL C. WEIL

ELIJAH WESBY

The First Six Officers
of the 555th Parachute Infantry Battalion

CLIFFORD ALLEN

EDWARD BAKER

BRADLEY BIGGS

WARREN C. CORNELIUS

JASPER E. ROSS

EDWIN H. WILLS

Desegregation and the Triple Nickles

September 14, 1940
Selective Training and Service Act is passed.

June 25, 1941
FDR issues Executive Order 8802, prohibiting discrimination in the defense industry.

July 1941
Air Corps trains first African-American pilots (the Tuskegee Airmen).

August 1942
Advisory Committee on Negro Troop Policies is formed.

February 1943
General George C. Marshall directs that a parachute company be created.

December 30, 1943
The 555th Parachute Company is activated.

January 1944
Original 555th test platoon begins training.

February 18, 1944
Original 555th test platoon earns their silver wings.

March 4, 1944
Original 555th officers earn their silver wings.

November 1944–April 1945
Japanese launch balloon attacks on U.S.

December 1944
Eisenhower invites black soldiers to fight "shoulder to shoulder" with white soldiers.

March 1945
Black replacements fight alongside white soldiers in the Battle of the Bulge.

May 5, 1945
Triple Nickles board train for Pendleton, Oregon.

July–October 1945
Operation Firefly

October 1945
Triple Nickles Battalion returns to Camp Mackall.

December 1945
Triple Nickles Battalion is transferred to Fort Bragg, North Carolina, and attached to the 13th Airborne Division.

January 12, 1946
Triple Nickles participate in a victory parade as part of the 82nd Airborne Division.

December 9, 1947
The 555th is deactivated and integrated into the 505th Parachute Infantry Brigade, 82nd Airborne Division.

March 30, 1948
A. Philip Randolph testifies to the Senate Armed Services Committee that African Americans would refuse to serve if a new draft law did not forbid segregation.

July 26, 1948
President Truman signs Executive Order 9981, calling for "equality of treatment and opportunity" in the armed forces "without regard to race, color, religion, or national origin."

September 18, 1948
The White House announces the President's Committee on Equality of Treatment and Opportunity in the Armed Services (Fahy Committee).

January 16, 1950
The Fahy Committee approves the Army's integration plan, after two rounds of rejection and revision.

March 18, 1951
The Department of Defense announces that all basic training in the U.S. has been integrated.

October 1953
The U.S. Army reports that 95 percent of African-American soldiers are serving in integrated units.

Source Notes

CHAPTER TWO

p. 8: "As first sergeant . . . something about it." O'Donnell, p. 106.

p. 8: "It is hard to identify . . . is dig ditches." Goodwin, p. 566.

p. 8: "to act like soldiers, not servants." O'Donnell, p. 106.

pp. 8–9: "We wanted to be a full partner . . . eat up the whole world." *Nickles from Heaven.*

p. 9: "The Negro should not . . . combat soldier," and "The Negro must be . . . moral qualifications." Colley, pp. 18–19.

p. 10: "World War I . . . who the enemy really was." Motley, p. 40.

p. 11: "draftees be . . . impartial manner," and "there should be . . . training of men." Wynn, p. 22.

p. 11: "been proved . . . period of years," and "would produce situations . . . national defense." Wynn, p. 23.

p. 12: "It seemed as if . . . awaiting any misstep." Wilkerson, p. 62.

p. 12: "contentedly pick cotton," and "dance and perform for their master." Bogle, p. 12.

p. 14: "They didn't make me . . . anything else either." Bogle, p. 127.

p. 17: "They could call him . . . now and was free." Wilkerson, p. 247.

p. 18: "I do hereby . . . or national origin." Franklin Delano Roosevelt's Fair Employment Act.

p. 18: "We have a lot . . . a pick and shovel." McGuire, *Taps for a Jim Crow Army*, p. 180.

p. 18: "On the post and off . . . in this slave camp." McGuire, *Taps for a Jim Crow Army*, p. 182.

p. 19: "We are treated . . . Please help us." McGuire, *Taps for a Jim Crow Army*, p. 191.

p. 19: "We're not even . . . a colored soldier." McGuire, *Taps for a Jim Crow Army*, p. 192.

p. 19: "a natural thing . . . an inferiority complex." Awosika, *Sarasota Herald Tribune.*

p. 20: "At four o'clock . . . we took over." *Nickles from Heaven.*

p. 20: "Within weeks . . . morale was up." Morris, "Baseplate."

p. 20: "An amazing thing . . . act like soldiers." Morris, Veterans History Project.

p. 21: "When you talked . . . in the eye." O'Donnell, p. 106.

p. 21: "They had found . . . white students." Morris, "Baseplate."

p. 21: "I was so nervous . . . sleep that night." Morris, Radio Netherlands Worldwide.

CHAPTER THREE

p. 23: "When I walked . . . scared to death." Trapp, U.S. Army TRADOC News Service.

p. 23: "tough as nails and just as straight." Morris, "Baseplate."

p. 23: "Explain to me what I saw," and "It occurred to me . . . might inspire them." Morris, Veterans History Project.

p. 23: "Now, I'm going to tell . . . top secret." O'Donnell, p. 106.

p. 24: "You'll have black officers and black men." O'Donnell, p. 107.

p. 24: "It was such a shock . . . my goodness." Morris, Radio Netherlands Worldwide.

p. 24: "My head was in the clouds." Morris, Veterans History Project.

p. 24: "My heart almost burst right there." Brokaw, *NBC News*.

p. 24: "I don't have any idea . . . my bicycle or flew!" O'Donnell, p. 107.

p. 25: "The Negroes are taking advantage . . . the Army." Goodwin, p. 172.

p. 25: "was not really welcomed by the military." Dalfiume, p. 83.

pp. 25–26: "We were able to get . . . on military bases." Hastie, Oral History Interview.

p. 26: "the most dangerous . . . United States today." Goodwin, p. 371.

p. 26: "Mrs. Roosevelt's . . . impulsive folly." Goodwin, p. 172.

pp. 26–27: "loyal Americans . . . ready and willing . . . Officer of our Post." Goodwin, pp. 421–422.

p. 27: "We do not ask for . . . any American soldier." Goodwin, pp. 421–422.

p. 27: "should be given a chance . . . to gain in the war." Dalfiume, p. 93.

p. 27: "this would create an impossible social problem." Lanning, p. 191.

p. 28: "no black units were to be included." Astor, p. 137.

p. 28: "The Air Corps brass . . . our proficiency." Goodwin, p. 423.

p. 29: (caption) "It was designed . . . not knowing me." Astor, p. 136.

p. 29: "As we left . . . racial discrimination." Goodwin, p. 423.

p. 29: "Where are your Negro paratroopers?" Biggs, *The Triple Nickles*, p. 3.

p. 29: "Blacks were asking . . . black paratroopers, too?" and "He let me know . . . all-black paratrooper unit." Williams, *Patriots*.

CHAPTER FOUR
p. 31: "I showed off my boots . . . I had them." O'Donnell, p. 107.

p. 32: "we became 'Triple . . . Buffalo Soldiers." Morris, "Baseplate."

p. 32: "At Huachuca . . . I became determined to get out." Motley, p. 62.

p. 32: "So here we stand . . . the first officer." Biggs, *The Triple Nickles*, p. 11.

p. 32: "We realized if we did it . . . the rest would follow." O'Donnell, p. 109.

p. 32: "We felt the pride . . . on trial every day." Biggs, *The Triple Nickles*, p. 20.

p. 33: "It was from daylight . . . three weeks of training." O'Donnell, p. 107.

p. 33: "running until our lungs begged . . . made of lead." Biggs, *The Triple Nickles*, p. 13.

p. 33: "They were trying . . . man-to-man thing." O'Donnell, p. 111.

p. 35: "knew that if he walked . . . airborne career." Biggs, *The Triple Nickles*, p. 17.

p. 35: "You would leave . . . three thousand." Biggs, *The Triple Nickles*, p. 16.

p. 36: "Keep your feet . . . go to the left." Airborne Jump Tower YouTube Video.

p. 36: "They looked to me . . . give it all I had." Motley, p. 62.

CHAPTER FIVE
p. 39: "Soldiers were fighting . . . segregated army." Krause, *National Geographic News*.

p. 39: "While in uniform . . . for the country." Astor, p. 215.

p. 40: " We don't any more want . . . your dining room," and "armed with bricks . . . the Negro welders." Goodwin, p. 444.

p. 40: "Those men . . . the post exchange." O'Donnell, p. 108.

p. 40: "sitting down at the . . . prisoners of war!" Morris, Veterans History Project.

p. 41: "a man who never met a stranger." Author interview with Alice Lowry, September 16, 2011.

p. 41: "There, in the South . . . I was black." Appel, *New Haven Independent*.

p. 41: "That irked us no end . . . treatment that we're denied?" *Nickles from Heaven*.

p. 41: "We were in one section . . . nothing to do with us." Morris, Radio Netherlands Worldwide.

p. 42: "We trained, ate, were housed . . . go to the counter." Beavers, "Conversations with My Daughter."

p. 42: "They didn't want . . . bring us our food," and "We had no recreation over there whatsoever," and "We were put in a hut . . . dead of winter." Audio Interview, Oral Military History Project, BMOH2.

p. 42: "Our rifles were empty . . . in the foot by mistake." Morris, Radio Netherlands Worldwide.

pp. 42–43: "I remember when . . . stooping to conquer." Hendrickson, *Washington Post*.

p. 43: "You could cut prejudice . . . smell it." *Nickles from Heaven*.

p. 43: "Be cool . . . shouldn't be wearing boots." O'Donnell, p. 112.

p. 43: "Both officers . . . they could be proud of." Williams, *Patriots*.

p. 43: "The general feeling . . . blacks would never jump." Andrade, *Retired Officer Magazine*.

p. 43: "because of the camaraderie . . . entering their special world." Biggs, *The Triple Nickles*, p. 19.

pp. 43–44: "would often go . . . racists on the post." Biggs, *The Triple Nickles*, p. 26.

p. 44: "We were determined . . . couldn't handle it." Biggs, *The Triple Nickles*, p. 27.

p. 44: "If you learn . . . tell you why," and "When he said paratroopers . . . my ears." Audio Interview, Oral Military History Project, BMOH3.

p. 44: "Curb your tongue" and "quiet your temper . . . ready for them." Biggs, *The Triple Nickles*, p. 5.

p. 44: "We fought segregation . . . It made us persevere." O'Donnell, p. 109.

p. 45: "D Stage was the real thing." Biggs, *The Triple Nickles*, p. 18.

p. 45: "a tangled mess . . . dug out of the ground." Biggs, *The Triple Nickles*, p. 19.

p. 45: "heels together . . . three-thousand." Biggs, *The Triple Nickles*, p. 18.

p. 45: "I remember every second of my first jump." Trapp, U.S. Army TRADOC News Service.

p. 45: "I guess I was . . . I would get relieved." *Nickles from Heaven*.

p. 46: "a lot of . . . that still quiet." *Nickles from Heaven*.

p. 46: "I slept very little . . . ever done before." Biggs, *The Triple Nickles*, p. 20

p. 46: "It was the moment of real truth." Biggs, *The Triple Nickles*, p. 22.

p. 46: "What is the minimum . . . using in combat?" Beavers, "Conversations with My Daughter."

p. 49: "Then why are you . . . black parachutists?" and "That is all . . . sent us." Beavers, "Conversations with My Daughter."

p. 50: "were really down on him," and "You know what . . . want you," and "But you've got . . . and hang," and "In that situation . . . out there by myself," and "It was rougher . . . encourage each other." *Nickles from Heaven*.

p. 50: "Technically, he was the first . . . the Army!" O'Donnell, p. 107.

p. 51: "When we got our . . . second-class citizens?" O'Donnell, pp. 108–109.

p. 52: "We got applications from everywhere." Williams, *Patriots*.

p. 52: "This was a chance . . . food to cadets." Hendrickson, *Washington Post*.

p. 52: "He was serving . . . godfather," and "And he said . . . need more officers." Morris, Veterans History Project.

p. 52: "We started combat . . . to go overseas." Williams, *Patriots*.

p. 52: "how to . . . fight as a company." Audio Interview, Oral Military History Project, BMOH2.

p. 53: "molded us . . . skilled combat company." Biggs, *The Triple Nickles*, p. 30.

p. 53: "By the time . . . fine-tuned combat unit." Biggs, *The Triple Nickles*, p. 31.

p. 53: "Upon completing . . . ready to go overseas." Audio Interview, Oral Military History Project, BMOH2.

CHAPTER SIX

p. 55: "With utter contempt . . . 'lynches your people,'" and "You might . . . heavy stick," and "You people are . . . make America better." Latty, p. 20.

pp. 55–56: "in America know a lot . . . me free." Morehouse, p. 8.

p. 56: "There may be . . . that Hitler can fix." Morehouse, p. 8.

p. 56: "If I was able . . . did not deserve me." Burns, *The War*.

p. 56: "I didn't hesitate . . . is greatly changed." McGuire, *Taps for a Jim Crow Army*, p. 173.

p. 56: "I just thought . . . treat them as citizens." Morehouse, p. 8.

p. 57: "I have to go . . . you can't deny me." Morehouse, p. 39.

p. 58: "Detailed and carefully . . . communications center." Biggs, *The Triple Nickles*, p. 50.

p. 59: "one of the finest groups . . . ever seen." Biggs, *The Triple Nickles*, p. 53.

p. 59: "the privilege of . . . knockout blow." Colley, p. 45.

p. 59: "the opportunity . . . to shoulder," and "without regard . . . most needed." Dalfiume, p. 99.

p. 60: "share the glory of victory." Wynn, p. 36.

p. 61: "They were all . . . glad to see us." Colley, p. 9.

p. 61: "seeing something American . . . Continental Army." Colley, p. 10.

p. 61: "I said I'd be damned . . . other boys to us." Goodwin, p. 567.

pp. 61, 64: "the greatest since . . . emancipation [of slaves]." Colley, p. 11.

p. 62: "It makes you feel bad . . . in the garbage." Hervieux, *New York Daily News*.

p. 62: "They didn't film . . . interview us." "Black Veterans Recall Their Roles in D-Day Invasion." *Jet*.

p. 63: "Where were we . . . in the history books?" Sherwell, *The Telegraph*.

p. 63: "We had to prove . . . we were the best." Nolte, *San Francisco Chronicle*.

p. 64: "the conditions under . . . most unusual." U.S. Army, Center of Military History, http://www.history.army.mil/html/topics/afam/aa-volinfreps.html.

p. 64: "At last . . . tangle with Hitler." Biggs, *The Triple Nickles*, p. 55.

p. 65: "the German armies . . . would be needed." Biggs, *The Triple Nickles*, p. 57.

p. 65: "We assumed . . . Pacific theater." Thompson, *Seattle Times*.

p. 65: "We were so happy." O'Donnell, p. 117.

p. 65: "Well, you got here . . . ," and "You were expecting . . . *New York Times*." Morris, Veterans History Project.

CHAPTER SEVEN
p. 67: "We had no idea . . . fight the enemy." Morris, Veterans History Project.

p. 68: "My teacher asked . . . scary, uncertain time." Sol, *On Paper Wings*.

p. 68: "I had the strangest . . . on me," and "there's only . . . are Americans," and "they threw us out . . . I cried," and "We had the face of the enemy." Kit Parker Films, *Beyond Barbed Wire*.

p. 70: "We had a mission . . . any other American." Kit Parker Films, *Beyond Barbed Wire*.

p. 70: "A lot of us felt . . . This was it." Ding, *The Color of Honor*.

p. 71: "Look what I found, dear." Webber, p. 232.

p. 71: "Don't touch it, don't touch it!" Sol, *On Paper Wings*.

p. 72: "We were all told . . . or anything." Sol, *On Paper Wings*.

p. 72: "an explosion of unknown origin." Webber, p. 231.

p. 73: "It was work . . . five layers thick," and "We glued . . . used for drying." Sol, *On Paper Wings*.

p. 74: "My education stressed . . . for our country," and "We worked . . . for thinking," and "Don't think . . . without complaining." Sol, *On Paper Wings*.

p. 77: "We knew we . . . entered our minds." Sol, *On Paper Wings*.

p. 77: "It must be . . . are developed." Webber, p. 263.

p. 78: "[We had to] trade . . . to do that," and "We've got a job . . . do it well." Smith, additional transcripts, pp. 458–459.

p. 79: "We felt it was . . . in combat." Motley, p. 63.

p. 79: "We were . . . we had to do." Thompson, *Florida Times Union*.

p. 79: "They could walk . . . like a cat," and "They taught us . . . to eat." Biggs, *The Triple Nickles*, p. 64.

p. 81: "You could have . . . start back up." Rufty, *The Ledger*.

p. 81: "The largest fire . . . jumping at once." Motley, p. 64.

p. 81: "We stank . . . upwind of it." Biggs, *The Triple Nickles*, p. 66.

p. 81: "We had to fight . . . fighting bears." *Nickles from Heaven*.

p. 82: "We worked . . . ate like horses." Biggs, *The Triple Nickles*, p. 66.

p. 82: "The area on fire . . . from the road." Awosika, *Sarasota Herald Tribune*.

p. 82: "These were . . . areas," and "We jumped in . . . get up there." Appel, *New Haven Independent*.

CHAPTER EIGHT
p. 85: "the reception . . . of the restaurants." Audio Interview, Oral Military History Project, BMOH3.

p. 85: "[We] found it difficult . . . would not serve us." Biggs, *The Triple Nickles*, p. 62.

p. 85: "were living in . . . southern attitude." Audio Interview, Oral Military History Project, BMOH3.

p. 85: "The townspeople . . . toward black soldiers." Audio Interview, Oral Military History Project, BMOH2.

pp. 85–86: "a man who . . . 'cool' to us," and "had to serve . . . was our lot." Biggs, *The Triple Nickles*, p. 62.

p. 87: "The smokejumpers . . . wonderful relationship," and "They told us . . . wonderful relationship." Smith, additional transcripts, p. 460.

p. 87: "The most we saw . . . fine bunch to see." Becktold, *World War II in a Wild West Town*.

p. 88: "I could not help . . . better than our own." Biggs, *The Triple Nickles*, p. 69.

p. 88: "perhaps we were . . . we might see." Biggs, *The Triple Nickles*, p. 70.

p. 88: "Upon arriving . . . the United States." Motley, p. 63.

p. 90: "We could not . . . was very few." Telephone interview with author, April 21, 2011.

p. 90: "the battalion . . . balloon fires." Cohen, p. 43.

p. 90: "We did find . . . further training." Motley, p. 64.

p. 90: "We found . . . of the bombs." Ross, *Wildland Firefighter Magazine*.

p. 91: "This was like . . . what to do with us." Thompson, *Florida Times Union*.

p. 91: "The Army had . . . so they refused." Shaughnessy, CNN.com, March 25, 2010.

p. 92: "General MacArthur . . . denied the experience." Telephone interview with author, April 22, 2011.

p. 93: "Why, I asked . . . and my people?" and "I was struck . . . better place to live." Morris, "Baseplate."

CHAPTER NINE
p. 95: "Black people in the crowd . . . greet us," and "I kept that . . . crumbled up!" O'Donnell, p. 118.

p. 95: "It was a heck of . . . sort of situation." *Nickles from Heaven*.

pp. 95–96: "Oh, you should have . . . a great feeling." *Nickles from Heaven*.

p. 96: "a mud pond surrounded by sand." Biggs, *Gavin*, p. 73.

pp. 96–97: "were billeted in . . . a scandal," and "did well . . . been given." Biggs, *The Triple Nickles*, p. ix.

p. 97: "color-blind." Biggs, *The Triple Nickles*, p. 73.

p. 97: "our Army . . . our society." Biggs, *The Triple Nickles*, p. x.

p. 97: "well trained . . . well led." Biggs, *The Triple Nickles*, p. ix.

p. 97: "General . . . to the 555th?" and "newest equipment and weapons," and "I'll see to that." Biggs, *The Triple Nickles*, p. x.

p. 97: "I walked in . . . had died." *Nickles from Heaven.*

pp. 97–98: "Everybody was crying . . . Triple Nickles colors," and "I finally felt . . . belonged to something." Gonzalez, U.S. Army, February 18, 2010.

p. 98: There's no question . . . nothing to do with it." *Nickles from Heaven.*

p. 98: "a symbol of . . . in the service." Biggs, *Gavin,* p. 65.

p. 98: "But he did more than that," and "Now . . . when you had . . . division positions." Audio Interview, Oral Military History Project, BMOH3.

p. 98: "moved quickly . . . officers and men." Biggs, *Gavin,* p. 74.

p. 98: "White soldiers and . . . racism—not one." Morris, Veterans History Project.

p. 100: "I was raised . . . myself," and "the vast majority . . . a free republic." Dalfiume, p. 134.

p. 100: "practice what . . . world was watching." Dalfiume, p. 139.

pp. 100–101: "We landed in Norfolk . . . so happy." Latty, p. 42.

p. 101: (caption) "We served . . . segregation." Telephone correspondence with author, May 6, 2012.

p. 101: "I had no idea . . . do something." Astor, p. 316.

p. 101: "When we fail . . . the whole world." Dalfiume, p. 139.

p. 101: "It is hereby . . . efficiency or morale." Executive Order 9981.

p. 101: "I am not asking . . . continue that fight." Astor, p. 322.

p. 102: "It proves what . . . American soldiers." Thompson, *Florida Times Union.*

p. 102: "the seeds of . . . were sown." Dalfiume, p. 106.

p. 102: "[African Americans] made . . . and abroad," and "It started . . . of their attitudes." Krause, *National Geographic News.*

p. 103: "I carried myself . . . people could tell." Morehouse, p. 196.

p. 103: "the civilian population . . . and discrimination." O'Donnell, p. 109.

p. 103: "The individual soldiers . . . led to acceptance." Pryor, American Forces Press Service.

p. 103: "Before World War II . . . what to do about it." Morehouse, p. 203.

pp. 103–104: "I came back . . . spun around," and "I wanted to . . . come with it." *At Cooper Union*, summer 2009.

p. 103: "We realized . . . they had education." Morehouse, p. 205.

pp. 104–105: "I would never . . . let them down." Buckley, p. 327.

p. 105: "In World War II . . . never mind being heroic." Roston, *Los Angeles Times*.

p. 105: "They said we . . . from the ground up." *Miracle at St. Anna*.

p. 105: "We didn't win . . . to do with his ability." Thompson, *Seattle Times*.

pp. 105–106: "When he pinned . . . with my life," and "I always looked . . . for other people." Trapp, U.S. Army TRADOC News Service.

p. 107: "I'm proud . . . who followed them." Gonzalez, U.S. Army, February 18, 2010.

p. 107: "They opened . . . black paratroopers," and "I'm not concerned . . . jump school." Gennaro, *South Philly Review*.

p.107: "Just as the . . . become paratroopers." Thompson, *Florida Times Union*.

p. 107: "When you look . . . doing their job." Awosika, *Sarasota Herald Tribune*.

p. 108: "I don't answer . . . All-American." Pryor, American Forces Press Service.

p. 108: "When the 555th . . . who were involved." Awosika, *Sarasota Herald Tribune*.

p. 108: "Anybody can join . . . green—anybody." Gennaro, *South Philly Review*.

p. 108: "We think it's . . . soldiers they can be." U.S. Army, March 3, 2009.

p. 109: "The man with no . . . has no future." *Nickles from Heaven*.

p. 109: "These three gentlemen . . . the course of history." States News Service, March 30, 2010.

p. 109: "It was so awesome . . . to their stories." Sosbe, USDA Forest Service, April 5, 2010.

p. 110: "There's a great . . . dignity and respect." Awosika, *Sarasota Herald Tribune*.

p. 111: "To tell you . . . we'll never forget." Cassidy, *Tiger Ted Lowry*.

p. 111: "We treasure diversity . . . makes us better." Pryor, American Forces Press Service.

p. 114: "We succeeded . . . great country's history." Brokaw, p. 229.

Bibliography

BOOKS

Astor, Gerald. *The Right to Fight: A History of African Americans in the Military*. Novato, CA: Presidio, 1998.

Biggs, Bradley. *Gavin*. Hamden, CT: Archon Books, 1980.

———. *The Triple Nickles: America's First All-Black Paratroop Unit*. Hamden, CT: Archon Books, 1986.

Bogle, Donald. *Toms, Coons, Mulattoes, Mammies, and Bucks: An Interpretive History of Blacks in American Films*. New York: Continuum, 2001.

Brokaw, Tom. *The Greatest Generation Speaks: Letters and Reflections*. New York: Random House, 1999.

Buckley, Gail. *American Patriots: The Story of Blacks in the Military from the Revolution to Desert Storm*. New York: Random House, 2001.

Cohen, Stan. *A Pictorial History of Smokejumping*. Missoula, MT: Pictorial Histories, 1983.

Colley, David P. *Blood for Dignity: The Story of the First Integrated Combat Unit in the U.S. Army*. New York: St. Martin's, 2003.

Dalfiume, Richard M. *Desegregation of the U.S. Armed Forces: Fighting on Two Fronts, 1939–1953*. Columbia, MO: University of Missouri Press, 1969.

Goodwin, Doris Kearns. *No Ordinary Time: Franklin and Eleanor Roosevelt: The Home Front in World War II*. New York: Simon & Schuster, 1994.

Kennedy, David M. *Freedom from Fear: The American People in Depression and War, 1929–1945*. New York: Oxford University Press, 1999.

Lanning, Michael Lee. *The African-American Soldier: From Crispus Attucks to Colin Powell*. Secaucus, NJ: Carol Publishing, 1997.

Latty, Yvonne. *We Were There: Voices of African American Veterans, from World War II to the War in Iraq*. New York: Amistad, 2004.

Lundy, William H. *The Triple Nickles: 50th Anniversary Commemorative Book*. Columbus, GA: Richard W. Williams Chapter, Host Chapter, 1994.

McGuire, Phillip. *He, Too, Spoke for Democracy: Judge Hastie, World War II, and the Black Soldier*. New York: Greenwood, 1988.

————. *Taps for a Jim Crow Army: Letters from Black Soldiers in World War II.* Santa Barbara, CA: ABC-Clio, 1983.

Mikesh, Robert C. *Japanese Paper Balloon Bombs: The First ICBM.* North Hills, PA: Bird & Bull Press, 1982.

————. *Japan's World War II Balloon Bomb Attacks on North America.* Washington, D.C.: National Air and Space Museum, Smithsonian Institution Press, Smithsonian Annals of Flight, No. 9, 1973.

Morehouse, Maggi M. *Fighting in the Jim Crow Army: Black Men and Women Remember World War II.* Lanham, MD: Rowman & Littlefield, 2000.

Motley, Mary Penick. *The Invisible Soldier: The Experience of the Black Soldier, World War II.* Detroit, MI: Wayne State University Press, 1975. [This is a compilation of interviews and letters that tell the missing stories of some African-American soldiers.]

Nalty, Bernard C. *Strength for the Fight: A History of Black Americans in the Military.* New York: Free Press, 1986.

O'Donnell, Patrick K. *Beyond Valor: World War II's Rangers and Airborne Veterans Reveal the Heart of Combat.* New York: Free Press, 2001.

Okada, Reiko. Translated by Jean Inglis. *Ohkuno Island: Story of the Student Brigade.* 1989.

Powell, Colin L., with Joseph E. Persico. *My American Journey.* New York: Random House, 1995.

Schoenfeld, Seymour J. *The Negro in the Armed Forces: His Value and Status, Past, Present, and Potential.* Washington, D.C.: Associated Publishers, 1945.

Silberman, Charles E. *Crisis in Black and White.* New York: Random House, 1964.

Van Deburg, William L. *Slavery & Race in American Popular Culture.* Madison, WI: University of Wisconsin Press, 1984.

Verney, Kevern. *African Americans and U.S. Popular Culture.* New York: Routledge, 2003.

Webber, Bert. *Silent Siege: Japanese Attacks Against North America in World War II.* Fairfield, WA: Ye Galleon Press, 1984.

Wilkerson, Isabel. *The Warmth of Other Suns: The Epic Story of America's Great Migration.* New York: Vintage, 2011.

Wright, Kai. *Soldiers of Freedom: An Illustrated History of African Americans in the Armed Forces.* New York: Black Dog & Leventhal, 2002.

Wynn, Neil A. *The Afro-American and the Second World War.* New York: Holmes & Meier, 1993.

Yenne, Bill. *Rising Sons: The Japanese American GIs Who Fought for the United States in World War II.* New York: Thomas Dunne, 2007.

ARTICLES

Aizenman, Nurith C. "Black Soldiers Battled Fascism and Racism." *Washington Post,* May 26, 2004.

Andrade, Dale. "Trial by Fire." *Retired Officer Magazine,* February 2002.

Appel, Allan. " 'Tiger' Ted Headed for Hall of Fame." *New Haven Independent,* August 20, 2008.

"Army Honors Triple Nickles Legacy at Pentagon Ceremony." States News Service, March 30, 2010.

Awosika, Mary. "Jumping toward Equality." *Sarasota Herald Tribune,* February 2, 2006.

Beavers, Clarence. "Conversations with My Daughter." Autobiographical essay written for the Triple Nickles website, http://www.triplenickle.com/beavers.htm

Bennett, Lerone Jr. "Chronicles of Black Courage: William H. Hastie." *Ebony,* August 2001, pp. 96–100.

"Black Veterans Recall Their Roles in D-Day Invasion." *Jet,* June 20, 1994.

Corbet, Mark. "The Death of PFC Malvin L. Brown: In the Interest of Public Welfare." *Smokejumper Magazine,* July 2006, p. 14.

"4 Airborne Groups Prepare to March." *New York Times,* January 11, 1946.

Garcia, J. Malcolm. "German POWs on the American Homefront." *Smithsonian Magazine,* September 16, 2009.

Gennaro, Lorraine. "Keeping the Legacy Alive: Two Retired Army Paratroopers Are Triple Nickles." *South Philly Review,* November 24, 2005.

Gidlund, Carl. "Black Paratroopers Were WWII Smokejumpers." National Smokejumpers Association newsletter, *The Static Line,* April 1994, p. 8.

———. "Intercontinental Bombing Targeted U.S., Led to Paratrooper Deployment as Smokejumpers." *Smokejumper Magazine,* April 2001, p. 21.

Gonzalez, Kris. "Triple Nickles Recall Days of Segregated Army." U.S. Army, February 18, 2010.

Hendrickson, Paul. "The Triple Nickles and Change: Black WWII Paratroopers Gather to Recollect Their Home-Front Battles." *Washington Post,* August 8, 1997.

Hervieux, Linda. "All-Black Battalion That Landed in Normandy, France on D-Day to Be Honored on Anniversary of Siege." *New York Daily News,* June 5, 2009.

Kersten, Andrew E. "African Americans and World War II." *OAH Magazine of History,* vol. 16, no. 3, World War II Homefront (spring 2002): pp. 13–17.

Krause, Lisa. "Black Soldiers in WWII: Fighting Enemies at Home and Abroad." *National Geographic News,* February 15, 2001.

Morris, Walter. "Baseplate." Autobiographical essay written for the Triple Nickles website, http://www.triplenickle.com/waltermorris.htm.

Murchison, Joseph L. "Triple Nickles Invites Smokejumper Members." *Smokejumper Magazine,* April 2000, p. 24.

Nolte, Carl. "Memories That Will Never Dim/Black Soldiers Who Fought Battle of Bulge Honored for Heroism." *San Francisco Chronicle,* February 16, 1995.

Pave, Marvin. "'Tiger' Ted Lowry, Who Twice Went the Distance Against Marciano; at 90." *Boston Globe,* June 29, 2010.

Phillips, Wayne. "Negro Minister Convicted of Directing Bus Boycott." *New York Times,* March 23, 1956.

Pryor, Mike, Army Staff Sgt. "Sixty Years after Integration, Opportunities Abound for Minority Soldiers." American Forces Press Service, July 28, 2008.

Ray, Tina. "Fort Bragg's Airborne and Special Operations Museum's New Exhibit Tells the Story of 555th Parachute Infantry Regiment." U.S. Army, March 3, 2009.

Ross, Paul. "Remembering the Triple Nickle." *Wildland Firefighter Magazine,* June 2005.

Roston, Tom. "Spike Lee Discusses 'Miracle at St. Anna' (and Obama)." *Los Angeles Times,* September 25, 2008.

Rufty, Bill. "Paratrooper Fought Two Foes: Enemy, Racism." *The Ledger,* June 11, 2010.

"Science: Balloon Bombs." *Time,* June 11, 1945.

"Seeing the World Through the Eyes of Ashley Bryan, Storyteller." *At Cooper Union,* summer 2009, pp. 10–13.

Shaughnessy, Larry. "Trailblazing Paratrooper Broke Color Barrier in Secret." CNN.com, March 25, 2010.

Sherwell, Philip. "African-American D-Day Veterans Celebrate Barack Obama's Trip to Normandy." *The Telegraph,* June 6, 2009.

Sosbe, Kathryn. "Triple Nickles Bring Smoke-jumper History to Life." USDA Forest Service, April 5, 2010.

Thompson, Allison. "Paratrooper a Pioneer for Blacks: Hyde Grove Resident Recalls WWII Ordeal." *Florida Times Union*, October 18, 1997.

Thompson, Don. "First Black Paratroopers Fought Racism, Fires." *Seattle Times*, June 25, 2000.

Trapp, Brian. "First Black Paratrooper Pins Grandson." U.S. Army TRADOC News Service, February 6, 2004.

Vernon, John. "Jim Crow, Meet Lieutenant Robinson: A 1944 Court-Martial." *Prologue*. National Archives Publication, vol. 40, no. 1 (spring 2008).

"What Next, Please?" *Time*, January 1, 1945.

Wilkinson, Jeff. "Pioneering African-American Paratrooper Fought WWII Japanese Bombs on Home Soil." South Carolina's *The State*, August 14, 2010.

Williams, Rudi SGM. "'Triple Nickles' Proved Blacks Could Jump from Airplanes." Special Commemorative Issue of *Patriots* Magazine, 1990.

AUDIO INTERVIEWS
Audiotape Interviews with John Thomas Martin, Interviewer, Oral Military History Project for the Moorland-Spingarn Research Center, Howard University.

BMOH1: Clifford Allen, July 5, 1990, Washington, D.C.

BMOH2: Clarence Beavers and Walter Morris, July 6, 1990, Washington, D.C.

BMOH3: Bradley Biggs, July 3, 1990, Washington, D.C.

Oral History Interview with Judge William H. Hastie, Conducted on January 5, 1972, by Jerry N. Hess, in Philadelphia, PA. Harry S. Truman Library & Museum. http://www.trumanlibrary.org/oralhist/hastie.htm#transcript.

"The State We're In: Operation Firefly." Radio Netherlands Worldwide, Jonathan Groubert, host. Interview of Walter Morris, March 3, 2011. http://www.rnw.nl/english/article/operation-firefly.

Walter Morris Collection (AFC/2001/001/2946), audio recording (SR01), Veterans History Project, American Folklife Center, Library of Congress. Recorded November 21, 2002.

MOVIES/TELEVISION

Becktold, Terry. *World War II in a Wild West Town*. A Production of the Pendleton Air Museum, 2009.

Beyond Barbed Wire. Kit Parker Films, 2001.

Brokaw, Tom. "The Home of the Brave: They Saved the World," *NBC News*. Aired November 4, 1999.

Burns, Ken, and Lynn Novick. Written by Geoffrey C. Ward. *The War*. WETA, Washington, D.C., and America Lives II Film Project, PBS, 2007. http://www.pbs.org/thewar/search_details.php?id=5381&type=3.

Capra, Frank. *The Negro Soldier*. 1944.

Cassidy, Chris. *Tiger Ted Lowry*. October 2009.

Ding, Loni. *The Color of Honor*. Distributed by National Asian American Telecommunications Association, 1988.

Lee, Spike. *Miracle at St. Anna*. 2008.

Nickles from Heaven. Steve Crump & WTVI Charlotte Public Television, 2000.

Smith, Stevan M. *Smokejumpers: Firefighters from the Sky*. National Smokejumper Association, 2000.

Sol, Ilana. *On Paper Wings*. Film Is Forever Productions, 2008.

OTHER

Stevan Smith. Transcripts of additional interviews conducted for the National Smokejumper Association film *Smokejumpers: Firefighters from the Sky*.

To learn about the kinds of parachutes that were used by the 555th, I read selections from Steven J. Mrozek's *82nd Airborne Division*, "A Brief History about the Evolution of the Parachute." Paducah, KY: Turner, 1997.

To learn details about the four-week training that took place at Fort Benning in 1943, I turned to "History of Development of Airborne Courses of Instruction at the Quartermaster School, 1947–1953."

To learn about airborne training and techniques, I used the War Department's *Basic Field Manual: Tactics and Technique of Air-Borne Troops*. Washington, D.C.: Government Printing Office, May 20, 1942.

Photography Credits

FRONT MATTER
pp. ii–iii: Courtesy of the 82nd Airborne Division Museum, Ft. Bragg, North Carolina

pp. viii–ix: Courtesy of U.S. Army Air Forces

p. x: Courtesy of Ashley Bryan

CHAPTER ONE
p. vii, 1, 5: Courtesy of U.S. Army Air Forces

p. 3: (all images) Critical Past.com/U.S. Army

p. 4: Courtesy of U.S. Army Air Forces

p. 5: Courtesy of the 82nd Airborne Division Museum, Ft. Bragg, North Carolina

CHAPTER TWO
p. 6: National Archives (357-G-203-4690)

p. 8: Courtesy of Walter Morris

p. 9: Courtesy of Clarence Beavers

p. 10: National Archives and Office of War Information (ARC Identifier 535607/Local Identifier 208-COM-13)

p. 11: Library of Congress, Prints & Photographs Division, FSA/OWI Collection, LC-DIG-fsa-8a26761, Lee Russell, photographer

pp. 12, 13: Library of Congress, Prints & Photographs Division, FSA/OWI Collection, LC-DIG-ppmsca-12888, Marion Post Wolcott, photographer

p. 14: (all images) Everett Collection

p. 15: (all images) Advertising Archive/Everett Collection

p. 16: (top) Photographs and Prints Division, Schomburg Center for Research in Black Culture, The New York Public Library, Astor, Lenox and Tilden Foundations/Image by Gordon Anderson, (bottom) General Research & Reference Division, Schomburg Center for Research in Black Culture, The New York Public Library, Astor, Lenox and Tilden Foundations/Image by Winold Reiss

p. 17: Scurlock Studio Records, Archives Center, National Museum of American History, Kenneth E. Behring Center, Smithsonian Institution

p. 18: National Archives and Office of War Information (ARC Identifier 535604/Local Identifier 208-COM-10)

p. 19: Courtesy of Ashley Bryan

p. 21: Courtesy of the 82nd Airborne Division Museum, Ft. Bragg, North Carolina

CHAPTER THREE
p. 22: Courtesy of the United States Air Force Historical Research Agency

p. 24: Courtesy of Walter Morris

p. 25: National Archives and Office of War Information (ARC Identifier 535685/Local Identifier 208-COM-222)

p. 28: Library of Congress, Prints & Photographs Division, Toni Frissell, photographer

p. 29: National Archives (208-FS-872-3)

CHAPTER FOUR
p. 30: Courtesy U.S. Army Signal Corp/Private Jim Buck

p. 32: (top) © Bettmann/Corbis

p. 32: (bottom): Courtesy of Carina Biggs/U.S. Army

p. 33: Courtesy U.S. Army

p. 34: © Bettmann/Corbis

p. 35: Courtesy of Airborne and Special Operations Museum

pp. 36, 37: Courtesy of U.S. Army Signal Corp

CHAPTER FIVE
p. 38: Courtesy of U.S. Army

p. 41: Photograph from the collection of Ted Lowry, courtesy of Alice Lowry

pp. 42–43: Courtesy of U.S. Army Air Forces

p. 43: Courtesy of the 82nd Airborne Division Museum, Ft. Bragg, North Carolina

p. 44: Courtesy of Carina Biggs/U.S. Army

p. 45: Courtesy of Samuel Robinson and Carolyn Carter

p. 46: Courtesy of the 82nd Airborne Division Museum, Ft. Bragg, North Carolina

p. 47: © Bettmann/Corbis

p. 48: National Archives (208-FS-1783-1)

p. 49: National Archives (208-FS-1783-2)

pp. 50, 51, 120–121: Courtesy of U.S. Army

pp. 52, 53: CriticalPast.com/U.S. Army

CHAPTER SIX
p. 54: National Archives/U.S. Army Signal Corps (111-SC-202330)

p. 56: National Archives (208-PU-120V)

p. 57: National Archives and Office of War Information, ARC Identifier 535598/Local Identifier 208-COM-4

p. 58: Courtesy of the 82nd Airborne Division Museum, Ft. Bragg, North Carolina

p. 59: National Archives/U.S. Army Signal Corps (111-SC-196106-S)

p. 60: National Archives/U.S. Army Signal Corps (111-SC-190120)

p. 62: (both images) Courtesy U.S. Army Signal Corps/General George Patton Memorial Museum

p. 63: (top) National Archives (208-AA-47U-6), (middle) National Archives (80-G-218861), (bottom) National Archives (127-N-9527)

CHAPTER SEVEN
p. 66: Courtesy of U.S. Army Air Forces

p. 69: National Archives (210-G-3B-414)

pp. 70, 71: Library of Congress, Prints & Photographs Division, Ansel Adams (LC-DIG-ppprs-00284)

pp. 73 (both images), 74, 75, 76, 77: National Museum of the Pacific War, Nimitz Education and Research Center, Robert C. Mikesh Collection

pp. 78, 79: Courtesy of U.S. Army Air Forces

p. 80: National Archives (342-FH-3B-42503-29888ac)

p. 81: National Archives (342-FH-3B-42495-B-30004ac)

p. 82: National Archives (342-FH-3B-42509-29990ac)

pp. 83, 90: National Archives (342-FH-3B-42512-29986ac)

CHAPTER EIGHT

p. 84: National Archives (342-FH-3B-42508-29999ac)

p. 86: Courtesy of Jordon (JJ) Corbett

p. 87: Courtesy of the 82nd Airborne Division Museum, Ft. Bragg, North Carolina

pp. 89, 91: Courtesy of U.S. Army Air Forces

p. 92: National Archives (342-FH-3B-42504-29985ac)

CHAPTER NINE

p. 94: Courtesy of the 82nd Airborne Division Museum, Ft. Bragg, North Carolina

p. 96: Courtesy of U.S. Army

p. 97: Courtesy of the 82nd Airborne Division Museum, Ft. Bragg, North Carolina

p. 98: Courtesy of the U.S. Army/Barbara Gavin Fauntleroy

p. 99: Courtesy of Airborne and Special Operations Museum

p. 101: Courtesy of Ashley Bryan

p. 104: (left) © Walt Disney Collection/Courtesy Everett Collection, (right) TM and copyright © 20th Century Fox Film Corp. All rights reserved/Courtesy Everett Collection

p. 106: Courtesy of Walter Morris

p. 107: Courtesy of Clarence Beavers/Edward Howard, photographer

p. 108: Courtesy U.S. Army/Photo by D. Myles Cullen

p. 109: Photo by Prudence Siebert/Fort Leavenworth Lamp

p. 110: Courtesy U.S. Army/Photo by D. Myles Cullen

p. 111: Dennis Brack-Pool/Getty Images

p. 112: (top) U.S. Army Signal Corps (SC-353469), (bottom) National Archives/U.S. Army Signal Corps (111-SC-631041),

p. 113: Courtesy of Bill Wischnewsky/http://www.5jump.com

p. 114: Photograph by Saddi Khali of http://www saddikhaliphoto.com

p. 115: Courtesy of Jordon (JJ) Corbett

Index

Page numbers in *italics* indicate images

Acknowledgments

There are many people I met throughout the years of research and writing whom I need to thank. Stevan Smith, what a wonderful surprise to be able to cold-call you and be showered with a wealth of information about smokejumping. Thank you for sharing your documentary interview transcripts with me and for pointing me in the direction of so many other helpful smokejumping folks. Wayne Williams, smokejumper extraordinaire, thanks for being so generous with your time and resources and for leading me to photographs I never would have found. Likewise, thanks go to Dan Cottrell. Your perseverance accessing the photos in that safe is greatly appreciated!

Ed Howard—retired U.S. Army first sergeant, Triple Nickle member, and paratrooper, president of the Airborne Historical Association—you are a dedicated and tenacious researcher. Thank you so much for providing me with a bounty of historic Fort Benning images as well as other valuable resources, for always being there with an answer to a question, and for expertly reviewing my manuscript for all things Airborne. Thank you also to Terry Becktold, Chuck Sheley, Ed Booth, Rafael Alvarez, Ilana Sol, Reagan Grau, Robert Mikesh, Barbara Gavin Fauntleroy, Carolyn Carter, Alice Lowry and her son Chuck Roy, Crystal Poole, and Carina Biggs.

To my family, thank you for being understanding when the dining-room table turns into research headquarters for far too long, and for being so supportive and loving along this journey we are taking together. To Sarah Aronson, for always having my back, being my best friend, and reminding me "you can" when I think maybe I can't. Thank you, once again, to Marc Aronson, Hilary Van Dusen, Sherry Fatla, and the Candlewick team for yet another wonderful collaborative project. An enormous hug and thank-you to the wonderful Ashley Bryan for sharing your words, your feelings, your art, and most of all, your joyous spirit. And to Susan Valdina for your ever-present love and loyalty to Ashley, as well as your expert scanning techniques!

A huge expression of thanks to Joe Murchison, who, in addition to reading the manuscript, spent an enormous amount of time on the phone with me and never failed to help in my efforts to track down leads. And of course, an it-can't-possibly-be-big-enough tremendous thank-you to Walter Morris, Clarence Beavers, and Jordon (JJ) Corbett, for reading the manuscript, allowing me to get to know you, and for simply being who you are—proud members of the 555th. Airborne Out!